ORIGINAL
PORSCHE 356

ORIGINAL
PORSCHE 356

LAURENCE MEREDITH

PHOTOGRAPHY BY ROWAN ISAAC
WITH DIETER REBMANN

EDITED BY MARK HUGHES

BAY VIEW
BOOKS

FRONT COVER
One of the last of the 'Pre-A' models, this cabriolet owned by
Paul and Janet Hough is a 'Continental' model, as sold in
North America in 1955 only.

HALF-TITLE PAGE
The very first right-hand drive Porsche ever made, this 1951
cabriolet has been impeccably restored and is now owned by
Porsche Cars GB.

TITLE PAGE
A highly prized icon among 356 models. The Speedster was a
cut-price Porsche in its day, but now it has become one of the
most valuable 356s.

CONTENTS PAGE
The fastest 356s are the Carreras: this 1964 Carrera 2 with
a 2-litre engine developing 130bhp belongs to the
Porsche Museum.

BACK COVER
The final evolutionary step came with the 356C, which
introduced disc brakes to production Porsches. This gorgeous
coupé is owned by David Griffin.

Published 1995 by Bay View Books Ltd
The Red House, 25-26 Bridgeland Street
Bideford, Devon EX39 2PZ

© Copyright 1995 Bay View Books Ltd
Typesetting and design by Chris Fayers & Sarah Ward
Sub-editing by Elizabeth Kirby

ISBN 1 870979 58 3
Printed in Hong Kong
by Paramount Printing Group

CONTENTS

INTRODUCTION

The years immediately following the Second World War heralded a new era in the history of the motor car with the emergence of three of the world's greatest manufacturers of sports cars. In Italy the first of a long line of classics bearing the name of Enzo Ferrari was born, in England David Brown bought out Aston Martin for £75,000, and in Germany the long-held ambition of Ferdinand and Ferry Porsche to build their own sports car finally came to fruition. All three manufacturers are still in the business of making some of the world's best and most desirable sports cars and continue to lead with their innovative and evocative design.

For the Porsche family, the resurrection of their company after the war could not have been a more difficult task. Germany had been defeated, its major cities decimated by Allied bombing raids, its communications networks almost non-existent and its economy virtually bankrupt. Various members of the Porsche family, including Professor Ferdinand Porsche, son Ferry and son-in-law Anton Piëch, had been arrested and imprisoned. By the time of their release in 1947, the Professor, now 70, was in poor physical health and mentally weakened by accusations made by the French authorities, who wrongly alleged that he was a war criminal.

The company's headquarters in Stuttgart were occupied by members of the American armed forces, and the team which had been responsible for designing the legendary Beetle and the fabulous Auto Union Grand Prix car now suffered the ignominy of having to repair and manufacture garden implements, old *Kübelwagens* and agricultural machinery. For the next two years, the future for the Porsche family looked grim, the successful years of

the 1930s well behind them. However, like the proverbial Phoenix rising from the ashes, the company was soon turning its attention again to the serious job of designing motor cars. Only this time, it would build them too.

Ferdinand Porsche had spent the greater part of his adult life working for other people. Before the war, he had penned many successful designs for Austro Daimler and Daimler-Benz, among others, and it had become apparent to him that his employers made considerably more money from his work than he did. By then well into his 50s Porsche was a pragmatic man who knew himself to be a gifted engineer, and he had no time for the bickering and internal politics of large companies.

The very first Porsche sports car. The 356 shape was established from the start, but this prototype, still owned by Porsche, is unique in having its VW Beetle engine mounted amidships, with the gearbox slung behind it. The prototype's simple cabin shields its occupants with a frameless windscreen. This car scored a class win in a minor road race at Innsbruck just five weeks after it was finished.

With lid removed, the mid-engined layout becomes visible (above). The prototype's dashboard bears little relation to the style used in the Gmünd-built cars that followed. An historic chassis plate (right): 356-001 is the very first Porsche, the start of a legend.

Against a background of world recession and runaway inflation, on 25 April 1931 he founded his own design consultancy, the *Porsche Konstruktionbüro für Motorenfahrzeug und Wasserfahrzeugbau*, which was willing to draught anything to do with transport – cars, trains, boats or planes. The small team worked on a variety of projects which included designs for small cars for the motorcycle manufacturers, Zündapp and NSU, neither of which went into production, as well as the Auto Union Grand Prix car and the air-cooled Volkswagen.

Porsche's passion was for sports cars and motor racing, but his dream to design and build one bearing his name was no easier for a small, impecunious company to fulfil 60 years ago than it is today. In 1939 he came close with the Porsche Type 60K10, a streamlined alloy-bodied 1.5-litre coupé based on the Volkswagen's chassis and running gear. Destined to compete in the Berlin-Rome road race, the 60K10 project was shelved after the construction of just three cars when the event was cancelled because of the war. Nonetheless, the Berlin-Rome racer is important because it marked an intellectual turning point for the Professor, sowing the seeds for project number 356 – the first car with the Porsche name.

The company's first design, in 1931, had been a 2.1-litre car for Wanderer, but because the Professor did not want to give the impression that his fledgling concern had not previously worked in the field of automotive design, it was given the project serial number of seven rather than one. It naturally follows, therefore, that when work began on the 356 on 11 June 1947, it was not the 356th Porsche design at all, but the 349th. Considering the old man's formidable reputation – he had designed some of the world's finest sports racing cars throughout the 1920s – this appears an unnecessary ruse, but Porsche was a cautious man who was aware that some of his potential customers might be suspicious of his inexperience.

Professor Porsche was still in prison when the numbers '356' were first put down on paper on 17 June 1947, and it was left to Ferry Porsche to steer the company through some of its most difficult days until his father's release in August. The first drawings for the 356 prototype were finished in July and the rolling chassis, driven by Ferry Porsche, first took to the roads in the following March.

This first Porsche sports car, chassis number 356-001, was a very different animal from the succeeding production versions. Produced in temporary premises in Gmünd, Austria, in what was once a sawmill, it had a tubular frame chassis, a smooth, slippery open-top body and an 1131cc Volkswagen Beetle engine which was mounted amidships with the gearbox slung out in the tail. To begin with, the prototype had a single downdraught Solex carburettor, but with twin carburettors and the compression ratio raised from 5.8:1 to 7:1, maximum power went up from the standard Beetle engine's feeble 25bhp to a slightly more impressive 40bhp. Despite the poor quality fuels available in Austria at the time, both Ferry Porsche and Professor Eberan von Eberhorst (Auto Union's development engineer before the war) tested the car and were able to pronounce it adequately lively.

Virtually all the mechanical components were Volkswagen, including the torsion bar suspension and steering gearbox, and their proven reliability meant that months of development work was not necessary. The shapely, curvaceous aluminium alloy body was designed by Erwin Komenda and constructed by hand in just two months by master craftsman Friedrich Weber. An invaluable member of the

Porsche team, Weber learned the art of coachbuilding while working for Austro Daimler at a time when Ferdinand Porsche was a member of that company's board. But if his strength lay in his great skill, his weakness lay in an affection for the bottle that at times held up production at Gmünd...

Built under the most difficult circumstances when even sparking plugs had to be smuggled to Austria from Germany, that very first Porsche, capable of a top speed in the region of 80mph, was completed by 8 June 1948, given the registration number K 45286, and presented to the motoring press at the Swiss Grand Prix. Just a few weeks later, on 11 July, Ferry Porsche's cousin, Herbert Kaes, scored an auspicious class victory with the car in a minor road race at Innsbruck. This was a welcome boost to a company which was experiencing hideous difficulties in its efforts to manufacture cars.

The old Gmünd sawmill was cramped, and miles from the nearest rail terminal. There were problems with securing capital and the supply of raw materials and mechanical components, and many of the tools needed to make and assemble the cars had 'disappeared' after the war. Gradually, these difficulties were overcome. Ferry Porsche struck a deal with Volkswagen's general manager, Heinz Nordhoff, for a regular supply of mechanical components and secured a royalty fee for each Beetle produced. In June 1948 the old Reichsmark was replaced by the Deutschmark, the economy was deregulated and the principles of free trade applied once more.

As production continued slowly in Austria, Ferry Porsche investigated the possibility of setting up shop in Stuttgart. The original Porsche works in Züffenhausen was still occupied by the American forces, so Porsche rented a small building next door, and took additional space at the Reutter coachbuilding factory. This proved to be a most convenient arrangement for both parties, with Reutter being awarded a contract to build bodies for an initial batch of 500 cars, while the Gläser company was instructed to build the cabriolet versions. Unlike the Gmünd-made bodies, the Reutter and Gläser bodies were made of steel to ease the pressures on production. It is somehow reassuring that the first Reutter body, produced by some of Germany's best craftsmen, was not symmetrical at the front and had to be modified subsequently! Orders for the cars came rolling in from Holland, Portugal, Sweden and Switzerland. Stringent import restrictions meant that they could not be fulfilled immediately, but at least the company was on its way.

When the Porsche Type 356 made its motor show debut at Geneva in the spring of 1949, the company had already sold its products to a number of important people, including King Farouk's cousin, Prince Abd el Moneim. The reaction to the car from press and public alike was very favourable because, apart

from the Beetle on which it was based, the new Porsche was so different from anything else that had preceded it. In fact, it was a revelation, for its design challenged the idea of the conventional sports car. The engine was in the 'wrong' position and was not cooled by water, the wings and headlamps were integrated into the body, there was no chromed radiator grille up front, and the Porsche's overall shape, based on sound aerodynamic thinking, allowed relatively high performance from a small engine.

The 356 was developed over the next 15 years until it reached the end of its useful life and was superseded by the six-cylinder 911, another all-time Porsche classic that, amazingly, still remains in production some 30 years after it was launched. But this Porsche story is about the 356, the car which to many is the classic Porsche.

First of line (above). With all-round independent suspension, a unitary body and a low drag coefficient of just 0.29, the original 356 – this is a Gmünd car from 1950 – was one of the most unconventional, yet advanced, designs of its day. Last of line (right). The 356C in 2-litre four-cam Carrera 2 form – the ultimate in performance from the 356 family. The overall form remains similar to the first cars produced 15 years earlier, but almost every detail has changed.

THE GMÜND CARS (1948-51)

By May 1948, a month before the prototype was completed, drawings for the production 356 in both coupé and cabriolet guises had been finished. In place of the prototype's spaceframe chassis was a more conventional steel structure built on the box-section principle, which was not only rigid and light but easier and cheaper to build. The engine and transaxle assembly were turned through 180 degrees so that the 356 became rear-engined like the Volkswagen. The first chassis, 356/2-001, was completed in April 1948 and its streamlined aluminium bodywork was made in June and July.

Despite problems with the supply of raw materials and mechanical components which delayed production, Porsche ordered sales brochures for the new cars from a Vienna-based printing company. The company's first customer was the well-known Zurich motor dealer and car enthusiast, Rupprecht von Senger, who ordered the first four 356s, providing Porsche with much needed capital. Von Senger also agreed to guarantee supplies of Volkswagen parts and sheet aluminium from Switzerland, and signed a contract with Porsche to that effect.

Production continued on a rather hand-to-mouth basis and before the move to Stuttgart only a small number of coupés and cabriolets had been completed. Exactly how many has been a subject for debate but it appears that, in addition to the mid-engined prototype, there were only 49 cars delivered to customers between August 1948 and September 1951. Usually, the coupé versions were built in Gmünd and the cabriolets were made by Beutler in

Thun, Switzerland on completed chassis delivered by Porsche. However, some cars were finished in Vienna by Austro-Tatra, and some by the Keibl Coachworks, the company responsible for building bodies for the Volkswagen-based Denzel sports cars.

Very few of those first Porsches, built almost entirely by hand and each unique in detail, survive today. Information about the Gmünd period is scarce and the difficult production conditions meant that there was little chronological order, with, for example, the fifth body finding its way onto the tenth chassis and engine numbers out of sequence.

Through all the difficulties, Ferry Porsche and his small team were trying to achieve the low-volume production of a sports car which would develop their existing principles. There was nothing new in the position of the air-cooled engine and the suspension layout, or the idea that an aerodynamically efficient body aided performance and fuel consumption, but the 356 was an exercise in fine-tuning existing concepts to suit the modern post-war era.

The chassis was fabricated from steel and was very light, yet so strong that it could be driven without the body in place. It was complex, with two side-mounted longitudinal members, a central floorpan and sturdy front and rear sections which also housed the suspension assemblies. A bulkhead section behind the front wheels and below the body's scuttle gave the chassis frame much of its torsional rigidity, which was such that the cabriolet versions required no further strengthening.

The many alloy panels which made up the two-

Presented to Professor Porsche in September 1950 on his 75th birthday, this restored but much used Gmünd-built coupé is one of three early test 'hacks'. It was nicknamed 'Ferdinand', the other two being affectionately called 'Windhund' and 'Adrian'. Having served as a factory 'mule' for many years, 'Ferdinand' was fitted with a large number of components more usually associated with later cars.

The combination of a rear-mounted engine and slippery coupé styling gave Erwin Komenda's bodywork design a 'hump-backed' look.

Early cars had a large, rectangular tail light, made by Hella and positioned above the indicator light. Except that it was coloured red, this indicator light was the same as the one fitted at the front.

door body were hand-beaten over a wooden buck and welded together. The 356's doors were front-hinged like the Beetle's, but the hinges were located on the inside of the bodywork, improving both aerodynamics and appearance. Opening quarter-lights were installed in the doors, a feature which was not carried over on to the later steel-bodied cars. Alloy bumpers were closely fitted to the front and rear and some even had gruesome sickle-shaped overriders 'borrowed' from the Beetle. Also from Wolfsburg were the large Hella or Bosch headlamps, but thanks to the six-volt battery that powered them they were no more use at night on the Porsche than they were on the Beetle.

Although the earliest cars had semaphore indicators in the sides of the front wings, the majority of the Gmünd Porsches had small round indicators which were slightly inset on the front panel below the headlamps. There was an alloy moulding strip between the indicators and some cars had a further piece of bright trim below it. An early version of the Porsche script was applied to the bottom of the front lid. To save money, the 'V' shaped windscreen was made in two pieces with a central division.

There was a pressing for the number plate in the rear panel and two small round tail lights which usually had a reflector on either side. The small engine lid, internally hinged at the top, was punctured with a longitudinal air intake fitted with a protective grille which fed cold air to the engine's cooling fan. Under the front lid were the spare wheel, six-volt battery, which was positioned centrally on the floor of the

luggage compartment, and 50-litre fuel tank.

The cabriolets produced in Thun and Vienna differed in detail from the coupés and from each other. For example, the Beutler cars had bodywork shaped more like the later Stuttgart-made Speedsters, a traditional steel windscreen frame, three dashboard instruments, a concave pressing on the rear panel for the registration number plate, and small, round tail lights and indicators, one above the other. The Viennese cars had just one dashboard instrument, as well as a frameless windscreen which gained its strength from a solid central division. These small differences serve to highlight the bespoke nature of individual coachworks, sadly no longer a part of motoring life.

Inside, the fixtures and fittings were typically spartan. In contrast to British sports cars of the same period there were no superfluous fittings, as one might expect from the designers of the Beetle. There was a large, three-spoke steering wheel with an ivory-coloured rim, a plain painted metal dashboard and minimal instrumentation. A large tachometer with a white face and black numerals sat directly behind the steering wheel. The Beutler-built cabriolets differed in having a speedometer on the passenger's side of the dashboard. Similar to the Beetle was the arrangement of the pedal cluster, hinged at the bottom rather than the top, a highly unconventional practice that was carried over onto the 911.

Usually covered in leatherette, the comfortable and fully adjustable front seats could either be separate or in a bench arrangement. There was an occasional rear seat for use by two small children, but in

Unadorned and underpowered. Porsche's ambition had long been to produce his own sports cars, but the 356's humble VW origins are plainly apparent. The front indicators originally would have been inboard of the headlamps on the front panel.

Early coupé and cabriolet interiors differed from one car to the next. These seats on 'Ferdinand' with exposed hinges (right) are from a later car, but this red interior shows the original Gmünd style with the hinges concealed (below).

practice this space was often occupied by luggage that would not fit in the shallow boot. The doors and rear quarters were covered in the same material as the seats. The door handles were mounted in front of the window winders and these were both pure Beetle items. Coarse woolcloth carpeting was fitted around the front inner wings and 'kick' plates and over the top of the sills.

The suspension system, like the Beetle's, had each wheel suspended independently by transverse torsion bars and trailing arms, with additional swing axles at the rear. Damping was taken care of with Boge hydraulic shock absorbers. The hydraulic braking system was made by Lockheed in Britain. All four brake drums were 230mm (9.06in) in diameter but 40mm (1.57in) wide at the front and 30mm (1.18in) wide at the rear. Twin leading shoes were used at the front, and one leading shoe and one trailing shoe at the rear.

Early Porsche brochures stated the engine's size as 1131cc (38.99cu in), but the cars were eventually standardised at 1086cc (66.25cu in), with a bore of 73.5mm (2.87in) and a stroke of 64.0mm (2.50in), to allow them to compete in the 1100cc sports car class in international events. Maximum power of 40bhp was developed at 4000rpm, sufficient to propel a coupé up to 80mph, a healthy figure for such a small-engined car in the late 1940s. Essentially an overhead valve pushrod Beetle engine, the Porsche unit had a higher compression ratio of 6.5:1 and was fed by two Solex 26VFJ carburettors.

From November 1949, all Gmünd cars were fit-

With just 40bhp and a top speed in the region of 80mph, the 356 was one of Germany's fastest cars in 1950. This car originally would have been fitted with a single exhaust tailpipe.

The legacies of this car's updating test exercises (below) include the Porsche crest in the centre of the steering wheel and a decent array of black instruments with green numerals, modifications that were not officially made until 1952. The simpler dashboard (below right) is more typical of the Gmünd period, with one large dial for the 160kph speedometer.

ted with revised cylinder heads. Whereas the Volkswagen heads had been restricted in having their valves in straight rows, the specially-designed new cylinder heads had their exhaust valves inclined by 32 degrees, which allowed an increase in diameter from 26.8mm (1.06in) to 38mm (1.48in) for the inlet valve and from 26.8mm (1.06in) to 31mm (1.2in) for the exhaust. This modification allowed the unit to breathe more efficiently and the power output rose from the 35bhp of the first production Porsche to 40bhp. The company's sales literature stated that it was possible to get 43mpg at maximum

cruising speed, but this figure could only be attained at low cruising speeds in top gear, which rather defeated the object of owning a Porsche.

Positioned in front of the engine and mated directly to it, the four-speed non-synchromesh gearbox was initially a pure Volkswagen unit with the following ratios: first 3.60:1, second 2.07:1, third 1.25:1, fourth 0.8:1, reverse 6.6:1 and final drive 4.43:1. Sensitive drivers found this crash gearbox rewarding but a handful of customers complained bitterly, and eventually an all-synchromesh unit was fitted in October 1952.

In many ways, the Gmünd cars were crude. The engine was noisy and there was little soundproofing. Narrow 5.00×16in cross-ply tyres meant less than perfect roadholding, but at that time tyre manufacturers were fearful of increasing the width of their products, as tyres wider than 5in were thought capable of imposing potentially dangerous loads on suspension components. Traditionalists quite wrongly blamed the position of the engine and the swing-axle rear suspension for the Porsche's perceived inability to corner safely at high speed. The 356 demanded a driving technique which differed markedly from that required for conventional cars, and few were able to master the early Porsches.

Strictly speaking, there was only one Porsche prototype – the mid-engined roadster which is now in the Porsche museum at Stuttgart – but in a way all the Gmünd cars can be thought of as prototypes, for they were built to test the marketplace. Even Ferry Porsche, acknowledged as an engineer with a flair for business, misjudged the number of cars that were needed to meet demand. Despite their relatively high cost, orders came in thick and fast and not all of them could be met. The only solution was to forget Gmünd and start again at Stuttgart, and this is exactly what Porsche did.

From the rounded fan housing to the fuel pump, dynamo and coil, the similarities between the 25bhp Volkswagen engine and the 40bhp Porsche power unit are obvious, but Porsche's first route to improved performance was through twin carburettors and larger valves.

Most Gmünd 356s featured this elaborate bright trim on the nose (above left). Luggage space under the front lid was necessarily limited (left), but generous by sports car standards. Because the car was not fitted with a fuel gauge, a wooden dipstick was provided for measuring how much remained in the tank.

THE 'PRE-A' 356 (1950-55)

Because Porsche's original Stuttgart premises were being used as a vehicle repair shop by the American army, Ferry Porsche came to an agreement with Reutter, the well-established coach-builders, to use a small part of its factory until his company's own building became available, with Reutter making the bodies. Porsche established an office at the family's former home on the Feuer-bacher Weg and the company's engineers made plans for work to commence in September 1949. By November, Reutter had received an order to build 500 bodies, a figure which Porsche predicted would satisfy worldwide demand. The Gläser company was also awarded a contract to build cabriolets from its new premises in Ullesricht.

The first Stuttgart-built car, a coupé of chassis number 5000 that was used by Ferry Porsche as personal transport, was completed by Reutter at the beginning of 1950 and differed from the Gmünd cars, which stayed in production until March 1951, in having its body in steel rather than aluminium. Steel was cheaper and Reutter did not have the skilled labour needed for welding aluminium. The styling of the steel-bodied Stuttgart cars was almost the same as the Gmünd cars but, much to Ferry Porsche's displeasure, there were slight differences

between the two. The few initial modifications mark the beginning of the continual development these cars underwent in their relatively long production career throughout which can be seen distinct phases which single out one model from another.

Production of what might be called the original or definitive 356 – colloquially known as the 'Pre-A' model – came to an end in 1955 to make way for the 356A, a model which led to the 356B T-5 in 1959, the 356B T-6 in 1961 and the 356C in 1963, with production finally ending in 1965. Not all of the modifications were especially important, and as not all were listed in Porsche's archives it is often difficult to be sure when they actually took place, particularly during the early period.

The development of the car also had its draw-backs. It certainly became faster and more comfort-able, even luxurious, but it also put on a substantial amount of weight, and however desirable the later cars are, it is the sight of the original 356, made up to 1955, that often produces the largest smile on the face of the dyed-in-the-wool enthusiast. Model years have also been known to cause confusion. The 356 model year usually began in September or October and ran to the following August or September, and naturally there is some overlap between

When Porsche transferred production to Stuttgart, the 356 differed from the Gmünd-built cars principally in having a steel body rather than an alloy one. The aerodynamic shape allowed a Porsche owner of the early 1950s to enjoy high-speed motoring without a large, powerful engine. At this stage the car had a single tailpipe. This famous car used to belong to Betty Haig and is now owned by AFN, the Porsche dealer.

A cabriolet version was available from the start of production, although coupés always proved more popular. This painstakingly restored car, owned by Porsche Cars GB, is the first right-hand drive cabriolet, and was imported to Britain by Charles Meisl of Connaught Engineering for the Earls Court London Motor Show in 1951. Like all Porsches built before 1955, it is fitted with 16in diameter wheels. The tiny rear window, glass on this model, was changed to plastic in 1953.

years. For example, some models will have been fitted with parts from the previous model year in order to use up existing stocks, making them difficult to date except by referring to the chassis number.

Like the Gmünd cars, the first steel-bodied 356s relied heavily on Volkswagen components. But despite this, and the 356's relatively high price of DM9950 (roughly £2000), Porsche had its work cut out making sufficient cars for a clientele that was hungry to spend money on good quality sporting cars.

BODYSHELL & BODY TRIM

Unlike the Beetle, which had a separate body bolted directly to a platform chassis, the 356 had an integral body and chassis of the unitary construction type, in which the steel outer panels were welded first together and then to the main chassis frame.

Made wholly of steel, the box-section chassis frame employed on the Stuttgart-built cars was

Two right-hand drive 356s competed in the gruelling Panamericana road race, and John Farrer's immaculate 1954 coupé is dressed to look like one of them. Detail changes by this stage included a one-piece windscreen bent in the middle, bumpers set further from the bodywork, and indicators placed beneath the headlamps instead of being set inwards from them.

Prior to the introduction of the 356A in 1955, several detail changes were made in April 1954. The handle on the front lid was modified and fitted with the Porsche crest, and horn grilles were placed inboard of the indicators. Colin Dexter owns this coupé.

much the same as that used on the Gmünd 356s, although the original Stuttgart Porsches were thought to be less satisfactory in their torsional stiffness. The reason for this is simply that they were mass-produced, as far as Porsches of the 1950s could be called mass-produced, rather than being built by hand. Parts were made in stamping dies, whereas in Gmünd the metal had been formed into shape by hand without sophisticated tools, resulting in an altogether stiffer structure. Not that there was much wrong with the mass-produced cars, and customers would have noticed little difference on the road.

Built in several parts, the chassis frame comprises two longitudinal box sections on each side (which contain the heater tubes), a floorpan in two pieces split transversely roughly in the middle, and a central backbone which, unlike that of Beetle, does not travel the entire length of the cabin. This shortened backbone arrangement could be something of a nuisance because there was no division between the driver and passenger footwells. Apart from providing additional strength, the backbone acts as a conduit for the brake pipes, throttle and clutch cables, fuel pipe, the rod linking the gear stick to the gearbox, and the wiring loom. At the front there is a foot panel, a vertical inner panel on each side of the foot panel, a strong bulkhead structure, two short chassis

rails with the front inner wings above them and a complex panel which houses the spare wheel and battery. At the rear there are two inner wing sections, a transverse panel that forms the seat or luggage area (which also runs into the small 'wall' behind the front seats), and a rear bulkhead. All the sections are made from sheet steel pressings spot welded together.

From a restorer's point of view, the chassis can be a nightmare because the entire structure is so prone to corrosion. Although underseal was applied to the underside of the chassis at the factory, it was ineffective, and virtually nothing was done to protect the inner surfaces of the box sections. The insides of the longitudinal members are also vulnerable to rust because, as they carry heating for the cabin, the inevitable condensation was not able to escape and so corrosion started virtually from day one.

The bodyshell was made up from a number of panels. The roof panel included the cut-out for the rear window, the rear wings were cut vertically behind the wheel arches and welded to the transverse rear panel, and the front wings were cut vertically just in front of the wheel arch and welded to the transverse front panel, the front scuttle and the top sill panels or inner steps. The lower sill panels running along the sides of the car had a distinctive shape and curve towards the underneath which remained

During 1955, most cabriolets and coupés bound for North America were badged with a 'Continental' script on the front wings. As an alternative, 356s sold in Europe sported a 'European' script on their wings. This badging exercise did not last long. This car is owned by Paul and Janet Hough.

A distinctive feature of the 'Pre-A' Porsches. The two-piece windscreen (right) was replaced by a 'bent' one-piece item (far right) in April 1952, and was fitted with a decorative alloy moulding at the same time.

Under the front lid the small compartment houses the spare wheel, fuel tank and Bosch 6-volt battery (right). From June 1952, the spare wheel was repositioned at a more upright angle to give more luggage space (far right).

unchanged until 1955. Towards the rear of the sill, there is a small circular panel on both sides of the car which can be removed if the rear torsion bars need to be extracted. All of the exterior panels were gas-welded together and the seams were smoothed off with lead. The only bolt-on panels were the doors, the engine lid and the bonnet, all of which were single-skinned but fitted over a steel frame for strength. An aluminium panel was fitted between the door and the interior door panel.

In contrast to the open-top prototype's drag factor of 0.46, the closed coupé had an impressive Cd figure of just 0.29, so smooth and aerodynamically efficient was the design. With its gentle curves, the car's distinctively feminine lines naturally aped those of the Beetle, but to sports car lovers it was altogether more stylish and impressive.

The 356s had a higher 'waistline' than the Gmünd cars, a slightly broader cabin, a raised bonnet and a more rounded roof and sides. The Sigla-made laminated windscreen, which was still made in two pieces in a 'V' formation, was lower and wider and the two halves were curved towards the 'A' posts. Driving an early 356 may have felt not unlike being inside a wartime fighter aircraft, until in April 1952 a one-piece windscreen replaced the two-piece unit. There were only a few minor changes to the body-

work during the life of the 'Pre-A' series, most significantly the slight change to the front panel (to accommodate revisions to the front bumper) and slight lengthening of the front wings that occurred when the one-piece windscreen was introduced.

The doors were hinged top and bottom at the front and differed from the Beetle in that the hinges were concealed internally, a factor which not only aided the body's aerodynamic efficiency but also tidied up its external appearance. Quarterlights, which were a feature of the Gmünd cars, were deleted from the door windows, but reappeared on the 356B in 1959. The coupé's rear window was curved, steeply raked and sufficiently large to allow good vision, unlike the Beetle of the period with its split window. The shapely engine lid, with two top-mounted hinges and a centrally positioned single air intake, was made narrower at some point during 1952. The air intake was fitted with an aluminium grille which, in essence, remained unmodified throughout the car's production life.

The front lid was hinged at the rear, and while the Reutter-built coupés had drilled hinges which saved a small amount of weight, those fitted to the Gläser-built cabriolets were left undrilled. The 52-litre fuel tank, with 5 litres in reserve, was positioned under the front lid well back in front of the scuttle, or bulkhead, and secured at the bottom by bolts until mid-1952, when it was widened and secured with metal straps instead. A large filler cap with a bayonet-type fitting was positioned in the centre of the tank towards its front edge. Before a fuel gauge was fitted in mid-1954, an appropriately calibrated wooden dipstick was supplied.

Apart from the small luggage compartment in front of the tank, the area under the front lid housed the battery (on a wooden base slightly offset to the right-hand side), the spare wheel (mounted near the front in an almost horizontal position), a simple tool kit and the jack. From June 1952, the battery, which was secured by a steel strap, was moved further back and the spare wheel was mounted at an angle to improve luggage space. From October 1952, the spare wheel was braced with a leather strap to keep it in position, and an alloy cover was placed over the battery area. The windscreen washer bottle was positioned to the left of the fuel tank. Originally made of glass, the bottle was changed for a plastic bag in October 1952. The washer was operated by a rubber footpump placed to the right of the throttle pedal on left-hand drive cars and to the left of the clutch pedal on right-hand drive cars. To protect the contents of the luggage compartment from rainwater, a rubber seal was positioned on the body – and there was a similar seal under the engine lid.

Generally, the body was devoid of superfluous brightwork but chromium plating was used for the headlight rims. Made by Bosch or Hella before April 1952, but only by Bosch after that date, the headlamps were exactly the same as those fitted to the Beetle except that the lenses obviously had no V-over-W emblem. The rear lights, made by Hella, were rectangular in shape with red lenses and had a polished bezel embedded in a rubber seal. The front indicators, at first slightly inset below the headlamps, were made of clear, ribbed plastic and had a circular bezel surround. Positioned directly below the tail lights, the rear indicators were initially the same as those at the front save that they had red/orange lenses. Absurdly small, these units resembled a lemon cut in half. The original type of stop light was positioned in the middle of the broad, chromium-plated number plate light housing above the number plate, as was common during this period. In October 1952, some of the lighting details changed. The front indicators were moved directly beneath the headlamps and the rear lights became two separate round lights placed side by side. The outer pair became the tail lights and indicators and the inner pair became the brake lights, while a reversing light took the place of the brake light previously fitted to the number plate light housing.

The elegant wrap-round bumpers were fitted closely to the bodywork along the bottom of the front and rear panels and attached to the chassis with

Twin round lights were fitted at the rear from October 1952.

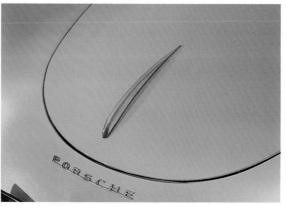

Porsche's designers paid extraordinary attention to the front lid handle. The first design (left) lasted until October 1952, when the handle was given a slot (below left) to make it easier to grip. A third design, much longer and featuring the Porsche crest (bottom left), appeared in 1954, first on the Speedster in September and then on the regular models in November.

The Reutter coachbuilder's badge, the design of which changed several times during the life of the 356 family (this is the earliest style), was fitted to the lower part of the front wing, behind the wheel.

Many sports cars of the 1950s were fitted with a rudimentary single-piece top, but the cabriolet's fully-lined hood was so well made that heavy rain and howling winds were never a problem.

This gold-coloured 'Continental' script appeared on the sides of both front wings of cabriolets and coupés sold in North America in 1955.

steel hangers. Curiously, the 'Pre-A' series had a number of bumper changes during its gestation period, the first type being flat with a central aluminium moulding, and generally without overriders. Grooved bumpers followed, and in June 1952 they were moved slightly away from the body and fitted with rubber inserts. In October 1952 they were moved even further from the body, a wider (40mm) aluminium moulding was fitted with a rubber insert, and valances were welded to the bodywork front and rear. Finally there was an interim bumper with 'A' style alloy mouldings and rubber inserts. The optional overriders fitted to some but not all cars did nothing to improve the appearance of the 356, but they had their uses in tight parking spaces. The early body-hugging bumpers may have looked elegant, but they were capable of causing more damage than they prevented, even in quite a minor front end nudge. The shock absorbed by the front bumper on impact was transmitted through the car, often kinking the bodywork in all sorts of unlikely places, necessitating an expensive rebuild of the entire front end. Until the advent of the 356A, when chrome-plated bumpers became optional, the bumpers were painted in body colour.

The chromed pull-out door handles were taken from the Export Beetle model but the alloy handle attached to the front lid was exclusively Porsche, resembling a section through an aeroplane wing. The handle was modified twice: in April 1952 it received a 'hole' on its underside to make it easier to grip, and in November 1954 it was lengthened and embellished with a Porsche crest.

In true German tradition, the coachbuilders' badges were applied to the sides of the wings. Reutter fitted one to the right-hand front wing only, whereas Gläser applied its attractive emblems to both sides for a while until eventually it adopted Reutter's practice of using the right-hand wing only. A Porsche script was fitted on the front panel just below the front lid, with the alloy number plate below this. A similar script was applied to the rear between the engine lid and the number plate light

housing. The V-shaped windscreen, rear window and rear side windows were secured with rubber seals. Unlike the door window frames, these seals were all without bright trim until April 1952, when a 10mm wide aluminium moulding was fitted to the rear window and the windscreen. The near side windows were fixed in position, but became openable from April 1951.

Horn grilles, fitted directly next to and inside the front indicators, had three chromed horizontal slats in the centre of a roughly rectangular surround, and were not introduced until May 1954. The windscreen wipers, with their spindly arms and short blades, were unmistakably Beetle items. Originally the wipers were of the 'clap hands' variety, but they were changed in September 1953 for more modern parallel items. A Golde-made Porsche fitted manually-operated steel sliding sunroof was available as an extra-cost option from 1954. The front edge of the sunroof was slightly V-shaped to correspond with the shape of the windscreen, and rubber drainage pipes to release trapped rainwater were located in the 'A' and 'C' pillars.

INTERIOR TRIM

Inviting and comfortable, the Porsche's interior was typical of its period. There were two separate, entirely functional bucket seats in the front, and an 'occasional' rear seat. Lateral support was lacking in the front as the backrests were fairly straight and flat, but the seats were adjustable fore and aft and were located in conventional runners welded to the floorpan. To begin with the seat hinges, which allowed the backrests to tip forward, were concealed under the upholstery, but after April 1952 all cars were fitted with fully reclining seats which had large chrome-plated hinges screwed to the sides of the backrests. The backrest was made more curved and body-hugging for greater comfort at the same time. A simple metal frame was used in the construction of each seat and springing was by coil springs.

In many instances there was no rear seat, the rear platform being covered in carpeting. Where a seat was fitted, it was either a bench-type cushion with an upright backrest or two separate cushions with an upright backrest. From April 1952, the rear backrest could be made to fall flat to offer improved luggage space, but the 356 was not an everyday family car and most owners would rarely have actually carried rear seat passengers.

The upholstery was usually leather or hardwearing woolcloth, but corduroy became a popular choice after 1952. Both the squabs and backrests were fluted and piped. The interior door and side quarter panels were usually upholstered to match the seats, and even the earliest cars had map pockets which ran across the full width of the doors. On the

Porsche interiors, these from cabriolets of 1951 (above) and 1955 (left), were typically functional. The switchgear, door handles and window winders are VW parts, and even the tinted sun visors on the earlier car are similar to those fitted to Beetles of the period. Note the later car's cranked gear stick, necessary because the base of the lever moved forward when the new all-synchromesh gearbox was introduced in October 1952. The later car is also shown with its rear seat backrest folded.

One of many changes in October 1952 was the adoption of lower rear seat cushions, enabling the back-rest to be folded forwards to increase luggage space (right). The seats were modified in shape in April 1954 to give better comfort and support (far right).

The early polished wood door cappings (right) were replaced in October 1952 by painted metal (far right), the colour of which normally matched the upholstery rather than the bodywork. The chromed door pull introduced at the same time was mounted near the front of the interior panel until September 1957, when it was moved to a central position. This later door should also have a full-width pocket.

Fitted above the windscreen, set in the headlining, the large courtesy light has a chromed rim. The original style of light (above) was replaced in April 1954 by one with a larger chromed housing and a restyled switch (below).

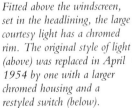

'Pre-A' series cars, the seats and trim were offered in a choice of colours including black, grey, green, blue, tan and red. Attractive wooden door cappings were used until April 1952, after which the tops of the doors were painted and reflected the interior colour. Like the Gmünd cars, the door handles and window winders were initially pure Beetle items, but from 1954 the window winder knobs matched the dashboard control knobs and were in grey, ivory or beige. From mid-1954, Porsche made knobs to its own design with colour-matched escutcheons, but continued to use Volkswagen cranks.

The broad sill area, front inner wings and kick panels were carpeted with a typically coarse but immensely hard wearing material that was glued and tacked into position. A large, one-piece rubber mat with a distinct ribbed pattern was used on the top of the wooden floorboards that were placed directly over the floorpan. In effect, these boards created a false floor over the clutch cable, which ran below the driver's feet! The main heater vents for the cabin were on the insides of the sills and there were two additional vents on top of the dashboard for demisting the windscreen. In late 1954, the dashboard-mounted heater knob was replaced by a rotating knob between the front seats on the floor, as on the Beetle. An ingenious system, both types of knob operated a cable which was attached to flaps on the heater boxes integrated into the exhaust system.

When the flaps were opened, heat was conducted into the cabin through the centre of the sills. The later rotating knob turned anti-clockwise to open the flaps and clockwise to close them.

During the car's early development, Porsche paid particular attention to reducing noise levels inside the cabin. Without the benefit of water jackets around the cylinder barrels, there was a fair amount of clatter from the flat-four. It was not evident at high speeds because the sound disappeared from the back, but at low speeds there was a tendency for resonance to build up. Porsche addressed the problem by applying sound deadening materials – tar paper and jute padding – to the inner wings, rear bulkhead and the sides of the engine bay.

The headlining on all 'Pre-A' cars was usually grey cloth but it did not extend to the windscreen pillars or upper 'B' posts. Beige headlinings made an appearance in 1953. The interior light, manufactured by Hella, was placed on the roof panel above the rear view mirror bracket, and changed in shape from domed to rectangular in 1954. A single tinted perspex sun visor was sometimes fitted above the driver's head on the early cars but after April 1952 a visor on both sides became standard. The interior rear view mirror in both the coupé and cabriolet was rectangular and on the small side, but differed in the way it was mounted because of the cabriolet's obviously limited space at the top of the windscreen.

INSTRUMENTS & CONTROLS

The upright Petri steering wheel had an ivory-coloured plastic rim with fingergrips on its under-side. The central horn button was also ivory coloured plastic, with a polished ring around the perimeter, and 12 wire spokes in three banks of four connected the boss to the rim. Elegant, even hand-some, the wheel had a pre-war look and feel and was most comfortable to use. In October 1952 a VDM two-spoke wheel was introduced with a new Porsche crest on the horn button and a circular horn ring. In April 1954 the wheel, along with the switchgear, became available in three colours – ivory, beige or grey – and the horn ring was reduced to a small segment. Ivory coloured knobs and steering wheels usually accompanied brown upholstery, grey knobs and steering wheels were matched to black or grey upholstery, and beige wheels and knobs went with red upholstery.

The detachable dashboard was painted metal in 1950s style, and had a distinct 'hump' in the middle. Instrumentation comprised a large circular Veigel speedometer calibrated to 160kph, with a large clock to the right and a small Motormeter oil temperature gauge to the left. All the gauges had white numerals on a black background and polished bezels. The glass covering the instruments was slightly dished.

The first style of dashboard, seen on the first right-hand drive car (above). Unlike the coupé, the cabriolet's glovebox lid has a lockable chromed button. Many 'ragtops' have the rear-view mirror mounted on top of the dashboard, but the Porsche cabriolet's mirror was attached to an elaborate bracket on the windscreen frame (left).

A Veigel mechanical tachometer, calibrated to 6000rpm, but not 'red-lined', became standard after April 1952 but with a clock still offered as an option. The tachometer was placed to the right of the speedometer. At the same time, the instruments were changed, with the numerals becoming green and the speedometer now calibrated to 200kph. A third type of speedometer, calibrated to 120mph and incorporating a trip meter, was introduced in late 1953 or early 1954. The word 'Veigel' appears at the bottom of each instrument.

Small warning lights were mounted on the dash-board between the speedometer and clock: red for ignition, green for oil pressure and blue for the indi-cator function. During 1951 they were slightly

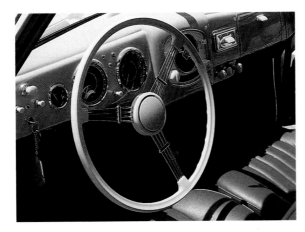

cancelling toggle switch on top of and roughly in the middle of the dashboard, but was changed in April 1952 for a more conventional stalk – a slim and elegant item similar to the one used on the Export Beetle – mounted on the left-hand side of the steering column. Switches for the headlamps, the wipers (which became a two-speed option from October 1952) and interior light were grouped together on the far left of the dashboard on left-hand drive models and to the far right on right-hand drive cars.

There was a blanking plate with a Porsche script in the middle of the dashboard which could be removed if a radio was ordered. To the right of the blanking plate was a pull-out ashtray and, on the extreme right-hand side, the glovebox which had a lockable lid on cabriolet versions. Initially, the glovebox was made of steel but this was changed for fibreboard in April 1952. Steel gloveboxes were lined with felt whereas the later fibreboard ones had a softer 'flock' liner. The passenger grab handle, present on all but the earliest cars, was a Beetle item mounted outboard of the glovebox. Below the ashtray were the heater knob (until October 1954), cigarette lighter and fuel tap, the latter operating a reserve of 10 litres. A pull-knob under the dashboard on the left-hand side opened the front lid, and another pull-knob close to the driver's seat opened the engine lid, released via a Bowden cable.

The pedals fitted to the early cars were rectangular, and in the case of the clutch and brake the arms to which they were attached were 'V' shaped, a legacy of being hinged at the bottom. The accelerator pedal was entirely conventional with a rubber cover laid over an elongated steel pad. Rubber pads on the clutch and brake pedals became standard after August 1951. The foot-operated headlamp dipswitch was to the left of the clutch pedal – in view of poor light capacity from the 6-volt electrics its use was optional! A little incongruous in a sports car, the steel handbrake lever was a pull-out umbrella-handle type with ratchet action positioned close to the steering column.

Mounted on the floor in the conventional position, the straight gear lever was topped with a Beetle knob with a slightly recessed centre. This was changed in 1954 for a Porsche knob, which was mushroom shaped but had a flatter top. In October 1952, the gear lever was moved 120mm further forward and was cranked more or less in the middle, a modification which coincided with the introduction of the synchromesh gearbox.

Ferry Porsche had set his sights on the important British market, and the first right-hand drive 356 was completed on 11 June '51. A coupé and a cabriolet version were first shown to the public at the London Motor Show in October of that year. That first right-hand drive cabriolet, which was imported into Britain by Charles Meisl of Con-

enlarged in size from 4 to 7mm, the blue light served for the main headlamp beam and the indicator warning light was incorporated into the ignition warning light. The majority of switches and knobs on the dashboard were from Volkswagen's Export model and were ivory coloured, with the exception of the black starter button to the right of the steering wheel. In the absence of a conventional choke, a hand throttle, operated by a pull-out-and-twist knob, was positioned to the right of the starter button. The knob operated a cable running down to the main throttle cable and attached to it with two metal clamps. To the left of the steering column, a switch was used for the ignition, operated by a tiny key. The indicator function was taken care of by a non self-

naught Engineering, was recently the subject of a five-year restoration for its then owner, David Mills, and now belongs to Porsche Cars GB. Modifications for the conversion were carried out to the floorboards and rubber mat, the steering arms, the pedals and handbrake. The battery had to be repositioned on the left and the inspection lid and aperture that gives access to the steering gearbox had to be moved, as well as the steering 'box itself, from the left to the right-hand side. The aperture for the steering column above the kick panel, the windscreen wiper motor and fusebox all changed sides and the dashboard was reversed.

WHEELS & TYRES

Made of pressed steel, the 16in diameter wheels were to Porsche's usual design with a drop-centre rim only 3in wide. They were fitted to the drums with five bolts and shod with 5.00 × 16 crossply tyres. The wheel bolts were changed for five wheel studs attached to the brake drums in October 1952. Initially, the wheels were not vented with brake cooling slots and were very like those fitted to both the Beetle and Porsche-designed farm tractors.

The hubcaps, which were secured by spring clips fitted to the wheels, were chromed from the outset and were similar to those fitted to the Beetle, naturally without the V-over-W emblem at their centres. Most of the very earliest cars had a ring highlighted in black at the centre of their hubcaps, but during the greater part of its production life the 356 was fitted with plain, chromed, 'moon'-type hubcaps.

Vented wheels (with 10 ventilation holes per wheel), which helped to reduce unsprung weight and cool the brakes, were introduced in April 1952, and at 3.25in were slightly wider. This minimal increase did little to improve either the car's roadholding or its aesthetic appearance. From certain angles, the body 'overhang', narrow track and narrow tyres made the 356 look a little odd. Not until 1955 and the advent of the 356A did the company increase the width of the rims, to 4½in.

After the introduction of the vented road wheels, early factory photographs show that vented alloy wheel trims were available as an option. With their multitude of angled louvres, the bizarre appearance of these trims ensured that few cars were thus equipped. Some wheels had ivory rims with the hubs in body colour, others had exactly the reverse of the scheme, but the earliest examples were almost always in body colour. By no means could the wheels fitted to the 356 be called sporting. They were cheap to make, strong and functional. The traditional wire or spoked wheels beloved even now of British sports car manufacturers like Morgan were not used by Porsche, except on a few early cars. The 356 just was not that kind of car.

ELECTRICS

It seems harsh but it is almost a mercy for Porsche's six-volt electrical system that the diminutive Bosch battery employed to run it is now quite difficult to obtain 'off the shelf'. Over the years, many cars have been upgraded to 12-volt systems, but naturally such a course is not original. Like the 75Ah battery, vir-

Plain 'baby moon' hubcaps were fitted to all 'Pre-A' cars, and ventilation holes were added to the 16in wheels in October 1954. Modern radial tyres have replaced the original crossplies on the later car in the interests of safety and improved handling.

tually all of the major electrical components were made by Bosch to the very highest standards and it is not unusual to find original dynamos still in good working order.

The dynamo, a Bosch RED K130/6 2600 A1 15P item, was positioned on an alloy pedestal cast in the right-hand half of the crankcase and was belt driven from the crankshaft pulley. The voltage regulator sat directly on top of the dynamo and had an automatic cut-out. Bolted to the fan housing via a looped bracket with the nose pointing to the centre of the crankcase, the coil was a standard Bosch TK 6/3 unit with its attendant wiring leading directly to the Bosch distributor, situated to the left of the dynamo pedestal. Secured neatly to the fan housing with plastic clips, the ignition leads supplied current to the Bosch W225/T1 sparking plugs. The Bosch EED starter motor, complete with a solenoid, was housed on the top right-hand side of the gearbox. The headlamp high and low beam bulbs were both rated at 35 watts. The tail lamps had 10 watt bulbs and the indicators, front and rear, were fitted with 15 watt bulbs.

Under the front scuttle, the small windscreen wiper motor drove the wiper arms through a metal linkage. The glass windscreen washer bottle situated to the left of the fuel tank was foot-operated by a rubber pump positioned to the right of the accelerator pedal on left-hand drive cars and to the left of the clutch pedal on right-hand drive models. It is unclear whether the glass bottle was changed for a plastic bag in late 1951 or early 1952. In contrast to the Beetle, which had its fusebox situated rather close to the fuel tank, the Porsche's fusebox was beneath the dashboard.

ENGINE

In the early days, Porsche had no option but to use a Beetle-derived power unit because it did not have sufficient funds to build an alternative. However, this simple, effective if highly unconventional air-cooled flat-four 'boxer' motor provided an excellent starting point for future development, for it was a work of genius which has come to be regarded as one of the classic engines. Purists may have derided the strange clattering noise which, at idle, sounded like a bucket of nails being clanked around, but for Porsche devotees the sound of the engine on full song has rarely been rivalled.

The 1086cc (66.25cu in) Type 369 unit, producing a maximum 40bhp at 4000rpm, had a 73.5mm (2.87in) bore and 64mm (2.50in) stroke, and a compression ratio of 7:1. It endowed these early steel-bodied cars with a top speed in the region of 80mph, impressive for such a comparatively feeble output. Installed in the tail and mated directly to the gearbox in front of it, almost everything about the engine's

design was unconventional. There was no sump in the accepted sense, the oil being contained within the bottom of the two crankcase halves, and unlike the majority of cars from other manufacturers, which relied heavily upon cast iron for the main body of their engines, Porsche made extensive use of light alloys.

The alloy crankcase was made in two matching halves split vertically on the centre line through the main bearings and bolted together. Initially made of cast iron, the four heavily finned cylinder barrels sit in apertures in the sides of the crankcase, held in position by long, threaded studs. These are secured to the crankcase at one end, pass directly through the barrels and hold the light alloy cylinder heads in place with nuts screwed onto their outer threads. Steel rocker covers are held in place on top of the cylinder heads with spring clips and there is a gasket between each head and the rocker box. There are no head gaskets. The short crankshaft which was made of forged steel and nitrided for hardness sits in four main bearings made of alloy and the connecting rod bearings are of lead-bronze. The solid skirted pistons in light alloy are fitted with two compression rings and one for oil control. Pistons fitted to the 1100 were domed, those on the 1300 were nosed and the 1500's were flat-topped. Because the exhaust valves are inclined at 32 degrees, the combustion chambers are roughly wedge-shaped in section.

Situated below the crankshaft, the camshaft is driven by helical gears and operates the overhead valves via tappets, rocker arms and pushrods running in cylindrical tubes, each cam operating two rods. The crankshaft also drives via spiral gears the distributor, which is bolted to the top of the left-hand side of the crankcase. The gear-type oil pump is housed at the rear of the crankcase behind a removable alloy cover and driven by the camshaft. The pump draws the engine oil from the bottom of the crankcase or 'sump' and pumps it through holes drilled in the case to the crankshaft, camshaft and pushrods. The oil is then pumped into a cooler which is bolted to the left-hand side of the crankcase. Concealed from view by the fan housing in which it sits, the oil cooler is a tall vertical structure rather like a residential 'skyscraper'.

Without water jackets or a radiator, the engine's health is dependent upon air drawn in by the fan through the intake grille in the engine lid, which not only cools the oil but also blows cold air over the cylinder heads, barrels and crankcase. Running at 2.65 times the speed of the crankshaft, the cooling fan is attached to the dynamo's armature shaft which is driven by the crankshaft pulley via a V-belt and two pulleys.

Hot 'spent' air is expelled at the rear of the car or used for heating the cabin by heater boxes integrated into the exhaust system. Air passes over the cylinder barrels and heads, is ducted via the heater boxes close to the front pair of cylinders through to the sills, and enters the cabin through vents in the inner sill coverings near the front seats. Hot air is prevented from entering the engine compartment by the steel trays or 'tinware' which sit over the cylinder barrels. A rubber strip between the trays and the bodywork provides a further effective seal against hot air becoming trapped in the engine bay and causing overheating. The condition of this rubber seal, and the correct seating of the tinware, is therefore critical. The exhaust system itself is one of the simplest, neatest and smallest arrangements ever devised. Made of mild steel, there are two short pipes, each of which is bolted directly to the underside of the two cylinders on either side of the engine. The two pipes are joined by flanges and clamps to a cylindrical tailbox or silencer, which runs transversely across the rear of the car. A single tail pipe exits from the tailbox on the right-hand side.

The diaphragm petrol pump is bolted to the left-hand side of the crankcase close to the distributor and is driven indirectly by the crankshaft via an operating rod driven by a cam on the distributor driveshaft. Petrol is fed to the two Solex 32 PBI down-draught carburettors through narrow steel piping. Apart from increasing the power over the original single carburettor engine fitted to the prototype, the twin carburettors with their short manifolds did not suffer as badly from icing up in cold weather, a problem that afflicted the Beetle with its long-travel inlet manifold for almost all of its production life. The oiled gauze type Knecht air filters sit directly on top of the carburettors, the throttle linkage for which is provided by a conventional rod system.

One of the great advantages of these early engines, apart from their simplicity, is their accessibility. As the 356 was developed, the engine began to fill more of the space under the lid, to the point where even changing the sparking plugs became difficult. But it was inevitable from the start that the 1086cc engine would have a limited production run. Although its size neatly slotted the 356 into the 1100cc international racing class, Porsche's customers demanded more power in keeping with the car's image.

Porsche won the 1100cc class at Le Mans in 1951 with one of the alloy-bodied Gmünd cars now displayed in the Porsche museum in Zuffenhausen. This was the first time the German company had entered a car for the French 24-hour race and it did so at the request of Charles Faroux, who had been instrumental in establishing the French classic in 1923. With its wheels enclosed by aluminium 'spats' and 44bhp available from the diminutive engine, the 356 was driven by the Frenchmen Auguste Veuillet and E. Mouche and had a top speed of around 100mph. This victory put Porsche on the road to

countless successes in international sporting events, including 13 outright wins at Le Mans.

Throughout the spring of 1951 Porsche developed the 1.3-litre engine (Type 506), fully intending to keep the 1.1-litre in production as well. The 1.3-litre, available from August 1951, is an important milestone – and Porsche's first significant move away from the original Volkswagen unit. Although the 64mm (2.50in) stroke was the same as that of the 1.1-litre engine, the bore was increased to 80mm (3.12in), giving an overall capacity of 1286cc (78.45cu in). Despite a lower compression ratio of 6.5:1 to allow the engine to run on any grade of fuel, maximum power rose to 44bhp at 4000rpm.

The new engine differed from the 1.1-litre in having alloy cylinder barrels which were some 2lb (0.91kg) lighter than the previous cast-iron items, chrome plated bores to reduce friction and Mahle alloy 'nosed' pistons. These modifications certainly led to more power but the light alloy barrels made the engine considerably noisier, although not everyone thought this was a disadvantage. To accommodate the larger engine, the cooling tinware was modified with larger cut-outs for the cylinders. Although the 1100 and 1300 engines were both fitted with twin Solex 32 PBI carburettors, there were differences in the way they were set and the figures are worth comparing. For the 1.3-litre car, the main jet was set at 0120, the idle jet at 60, the air correction jet at 240, the venturi at 24, and the accelerator pump jet at 55. The corresponding figures for the 1.1-litre car are 0110, 60, 230, 23 and 50.

Later in the year, an optional 1.5-litre unit became available. In August 1951 Porsche had entered the Liège-Rome-Liège Rally with an 1100 for Huschke von Hanstein and Petermax Müller and a 1500 for Paul von Guilleaume and Count von der Muhle. Porsche was cautious about the bad publicity a failure of its new engine in the rally might bring. The company even claimed that the car driven by von Guilleaume and von der Muhle was a 1300, but few who knew the 356 well and who watched this performance were fooled as to what was really under the engine lid. When the car finished third overall and won the 1500 class, it became obvious that Porsche had a new trick up its sleeve.

The 1500 engine did not become generally available to the public until March 1952, when the company announced its new line-up for that year. In the race and rally cars of that period, this 1488cc engine (90.77cu in) developed 72bhp at 5100rpm with a compression ratio of 7.4:1 and a bore and stroke of 80mm × 74mm (3.12in × 2.89in). Like the 1300, it had alloy cylinder barrels and chrome-plated bores, but for competition use there was a Hirth roller-bearing crankshaft in place of the plain-bearing unit, sodium-filled valves to improve heat dissipation, a 'hotter' camshaft (designed by engine 'guru' Dr

The original 1.1-litre engine was joined by a 1.3-litre in 1951 and a 1.5-litre in 1952. Based on the Porsche-designed, air-cooled flat-four Volkswagen unit, Porsche engines had reworked cylinder heads for improved breathing and were fitted with twin Solex carburettors.

Ernst Fuhrmann) and twin Solex PBIC 40 carburettors. Fitted in one of Porsche's 'old' alloy-bodied Gmünd coupés, this competition engine gave the car a maximum speed of more than 100mph.

From October 1952, the Porsche owner's manual cites four different engine options for the production 356. The 1.1-litre (Type 369), still available despite relatively low demand, the popular 1300 (Type 506), and two versions of the 1500: the plain-bearing unit (Type 546) and the 1500S (Type 528) with a roller-bearing crankshaft. The standard 1500 engine developed a a maximum 55bhp at 4400rpm with a compression ratio of 7:1. Light alloy was used for the main bearings with lead-bronze for the connecting rod bearings, the main bearing clearance was .002in to .004in, and the engine was fed by two Solex 32 PBI carburettors. The 1500 'Super' or 1500S engine shared the same internal dimensions but developed 70bhp at a maximum 5000rpm. The compression ratio was increased to 8.2:1 and larger 40 PBIC Solex carburettors were fitted. The Super's roller-bearing crankshaft (with a bearing clearance of .001

to .003in) was a complex piece of equipment made in 13 separate pieces. This engine was particularly smooth in use and made the 356 easier to drive, but its ability to achieve relatively high revs meant that it was never very long lived, often leading to a total and expensive engine overhaul after 30,000 miles.

When *Road & Track* magazine tested the 1500S version in 1952 it judged the new engine to be remarkable: 'It goes so easily. At 3500rpm, or 77mph, the engine seems to loaf along. The driver has no impression of urging the car in order to maintain high speeds. As a matter of fact, with its short stroke, the engine reaches 2500 feet per minute speed somewhere in the region of a theoretical 130mph. If we accept the dictum that 2500rpm is the safe rate of piston travel for maximum cruising speeds in a passenger car, it is difficult to understand how one could go about over-revving the admirable horizontally opposed four-cylinder air-cooled engine.'

From October 1952, a detuned 1500 version became available for ordinary road use. It had a forged one-piece crankshaft, a Volkswagen camshaft and produced just 55bhp. The 70bhp roller-bearing engine fitted with the Fuhrmann-designed camshaft then became available to special order. At the Paris Motor Show in October 1953, Porsche announced yet another engine variant. So that racing drivers could compete with 356s in the 1300 class, the company offered a 1.3-litre Super engine which, like the 1500S, had a roller-bearing crankshaft. The size of 1290cc was achieved with a bore of 74.5mm and a stroke of 74mm and the unit developed a maximum 60bhp at 5500rpm. Two Solex 32PBI carburettors were fitted and a relatively high compression ratio of 8.2:1 was used.

Because the 356 was so well shaped and aerodynamically sound, the fuel consumption of all these engines was exceptionally good. Even the 1500S engine was capable of returning up to 25mpg, not under race conditions of course but at least the car could be driven to and from an event fairly economically. In its road test of November 1953, *The Autocar* recorded 28mpg for the standard 1500 over 784 miles, with a top speed of 91mph and a best 0-60mph time of 17.0sec.

By the end of 1953, Porsche was not only enjoying some success in national and international competition, but also an upsurge in sales. Whereas the company sold 1069 coupés and cabriolets in 1951, the figure for 1953 rose to 1941 (1547 coupés and 394 cabriolets). The range of five engines gave customers plenty of choice, although the purchase price was higher. However, as the cars were almost entirely hand-built in such relatively small numbers, most owners considered their money well spent. *The Autocar* concluded, 'For the driver who wants a car which is different, albeit expensive, with import duty and British import tax added, the Porsche has a definite appeal. It is fast and comfortable, is well made, and the general finish of the fittings, upholstery and paintwork is an example of how thorough the Germans can be.'

Gradually, the 356 became less of a Volkswagen and more of a Porsche. Although the Porsche engines were more powerful than the 25bhp and 30bhp units fitted to Beetles in the 1950s, they had been little more than reworked versions. That all changed in November 1954 when all engine variants (except the 1.1-litre which was dropped from the range) were substantially modified.

Although the basic configuration of an air-cooled flat-four layout was retained, sweeping changes were made to virtually all of the components with the general idea of increasing strength. With the more powerful engines in the range, the original Volkswagen two-piece crankcase was put under considerable strain and so this was replaced by a new three-piece silicon-aluminium alloy crankcase. This was still in two halves, split down the middle as before, but there

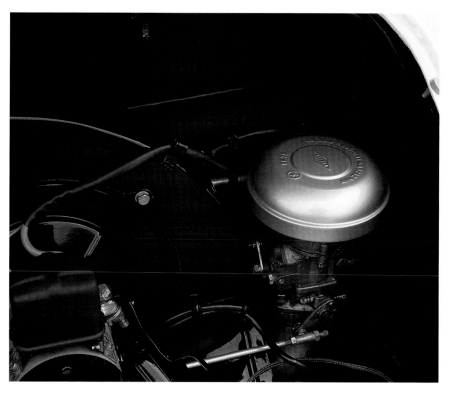

was also a crankcase cover fitted to the rear of the engine with a detachable dynamo pedestal directly on top of it. Previously, the dynamo pedestal had been cast into the right-hand half of the crankcase like the Beetle's. The new arrangement made life easier for Porsche in assembling the engines, and made the dynamo and cooling fan more accessible.

A new oil filler neck with an attached breather pipe was attached to the outside of the pedestal. Even the oil filler lid itself was modified to flip up for quick release: Porsche was not slow to learn from its motor racing activities. Other modifications to the crankcase included new supports on each side for the exhaust's heater boxes and ribs in the crankcase cover to improve cooling efficiency. The oil strainer at the base of the crankcase was enlarged and became rectangular rather than being circular in Beetle fashion. The oil pump was also increased in size and the oil temperature sender, which had been integral with the dipstick, was modified so that it was firmly embedded in the crankcase. The rocker arms were now made in two pieces rather than three and, because the fan belt was made a little narrower than before, both the crankshaft and dynamo pulley wheels were modified accordingly.

By 1955, the 356 had been developed to a point where the car had become one of the world's most respected sporting machines – quite remarkable considering the company had yet to celebrate its tenth anniversary. Porsche's policy of making modifications exactly where and when they were needed paid off. Between 1954 and 1955, production more than doubled.

The twin Solex 32 PBI carburettors not only increased the power of the Beetle-derived engine, but their short inlet manifolds also cured the 'icing-up' problem that afflicted the Beetle, with its single carburettor and long-travel manifold.

TRANSMISSION

One of the many endearing features of the early 356 was its non-synchromesh four-speed gearbox. It was an absolute delight to use once mastered, and changes could be accomplished almost as quickly as the proverbial hot knife through butter. Time the cogs incorrectly, though, and the usual crunching noises associated with these quaint pre-war artefacts would result. A Volkswagen unit, the gearbox has a two-piece alloy casing ribbed for both strength and cooling. Like the engine, the case is split vertically and longitudinally through the centre line and bolted together.

Bolted to the front of the engine with four bolts and to rear of the chassis pan, the gearbox is protected from vibration and engine torque by rubber mountings, and driven by the engine through a splined input shaft. Apart from providing a convenient mounting point for the starter motor, which sits on the top right-hand side, the gearbox also houses the differential and final drive. The latter sits between the clutch and the gearbox. It is a transaxle assembly in which the differential comprises a housing with housing covers, side gears, pinions with pinion shafts, and solid driveshafts articulated on their inner ends with flat 'ear' joints.

The axle shafts, flattened on their inner ends, are fitted between fulcrum plates in the side gears. The ear joints move in an arc because of the sliding nature of the axles between the fulcrum plates which work in conjunction with the rocking of the fulcrum plates in the side gears. Operated by a cable, the single dry-plate 180mm Fichtel & Sachs clutch, the same as those supplied to Wolfsburg for the Beetle, is splined to the gearbox input shaft. The clutch release arm was lengthened in 1955 to reduce the pedal pressure required when changing gear. As the gearbox was the same one employed in the Gmünd cars, the ratios were unchanged, as follows: first 3.60:1, second 2.07:1, third 1.25:1, fourth 0.80:1, reverse 6.60:1 and final drive 4.43:1.

So many customers questioned the use of an old-fashioned 'crash' gearbox that Porsche mooted the idea of an all-synchromesh unit as early as 1951. Developed by Getrag of Ludwigsburg, the new gearbox had synchromesh on all four forward speeds and was introduced in October 1952. Designed along the lines of the five-speed gearbox developed for the Cisitalia racing car during 1946-47, it used a servo ring system designed by Leopold Schmid, an Austrian engineer who had worked for Porsche from the early days of the war.

The Porsche synchromesh system was unconventional in that it did not rely on cones, but on an intermediate servo synchronising ring, where each pinion is fitted with a servo ring that revolves at the same speed as the gear. Made of hardened chrome molybdenum steel, each ring has a bevelled outer edge that feeds into a pressure face. When the gearchange fork at the rear of the 'box is moved by the action of changing gear, the clutch ring is moved towards the gear with the servo ring, and thus the difference in speed between the output shaft and the engaged gear is brought into line. The disadvantage of a conventional cone system is that changes can never be accomplished as quickly because the acceleration or braking of the gears takes so much longer at high speed. With the Porsche ring system, gear changes are so much faster because a servo effect is created by a synchroclutch sleeve.

The ratios of the new gearbox were as follows: first 3.18:1, second 1.76:1, third 1.13:1, fourth 0.815:1, reverse 3.56:1 and final drive 4.375:1. The new gearbox also meant that the gear lever itself had to be bent backwards in the middle and positioned 120mm further forward on the floor, a move which also necessitated a slight change to the rod linkage from the gear stick to the 'box and a number of chassis modifications. The gearchange was always to the familiar 'H' pattern.

In his autobiography *Cars are my Life*, Ferry Porsche describes how although his company assembled the new gearboxes, Getrag actually manufactured the components: 'At that time turnover tax had to be paid on every component produced and supplied, so if Getrag had obtained the individual components from the various suppliers and assembled them, turnover tax would have to be paid several times, making the final product unnecessarily more expensive. We were able to get round this by assembling the gearbox ourselves.'

SUSPENSION

Springing is by torsion bars front and rear, and the metal tubes housing the torsion bars are welded directly to the main chassis frame. At the front two tubes, one on top of the other, run transversely across the car, each having six torsion leaves. Two roughly parallel trailing arms on each side are bolted to the outer ends of the torsion springs. The trailing arms are connected to the hub assemblies via a king pin and two link pins on each side, and held in place by bolts. A rubber buffer between the trailing arms was fitted to prevent excessive up and down travel. Damping was by double-acting telescopic shock absorbers mounted vertically on steel uprights welded to the torsion bar tubes.

The rear torsion bars differ in that there is a single solid bar on each side rather than a series of torsion leaves. Contained within transversely mounted tubes located slightly forward of the gearbox, but behind the jacking points, each torsion bar is splined on its outer end and connected to a radius arm which locates the rear hub and the infamous swinging half-

The straight gear stick used with the original non-synchromesh gearbox was superseded by a cranked design when the all-synchromesh gearbox arrived in October 1952.

axles. This form of springing, patented by Porsche in 1931, was used both on the Beetle and the pre-war Auto Union Grand Prix car and had the advantage of suspending all four wheels independently. Damping was initially by lever type shock absorbers mounted at an angle rather than vertically.

The system was simple, incredibly durable and gave excellent ride quality over the poorest road surfaces. However, the supposed vagaries of the swing-axles came in for harsh criticism. During hard, fast cornering, there was a tendency for a rear wheel to develop the dreaded 'tuck-in' position and cause the car to oversteer viciously, or even, in theory, to flip it on its roof. Certainly, the Porsche was naturally tail-happy and it was possible to lose the rear end, but only at ridiculously high speeds. Driving a Porsche 356 was never anything less than rewarding for those who learned how, but not everyone – including some reactionary journalists – seemed able to master the new technique required to conduct a 356 safely.

Denis Jenkinson put it very succinctly when he discussed the 356 in *Motor Sport* magazine in 1955: 'I have met lots of people who have tried a Porsche and thought it terrible and when I have seen them driving a conventional car I understand why; they just cannot drive properly anyway.'

Suspension modifications were phased in gradually. The lever type rear shock absorbers were changed for telescopics in April 1951, and the throttle cable was changed for a metal rod linkage in April 1952. In October 1952, a number of detail changes coincided with the introduction of the new synchromesh gearbox: the panel that forms the rear luggage bay and the rear part of the backbone tunnel were modified, and the apertures through which the clutch and starter cables were routed had to be moved to accommodate the synchromesh gearbox.

Usefully, a front anti-roll bar was added in November 1954 and went a little way towards improving the roadholding by reducing the car's tendency to oversteer. It was a much appreciated modification which allowed an enthusiastic driver to reach even higher speeds in the corners before the tail started to step out of line, but criticism of the handling continued. In the following extract from his article in *Sports Club of America*, the Porsche racing driver, Richard von Frankenberg, defends the car by explaining perfectly the manner in which a 356 should be driven safely at high speeds.

'Often it is said that the Porsche is a difficult car to steer at high speed. In my opinion, this does not hold true. It must be admitted, however, that the Porsche must be driven with a different technique than the normal front-engined car. This different 'technique' one has, so to speak, to learn. The Porsche is a car which announces in time when it reaches the limit of road adhesion and it is for this reason that I find if easier to drive than a normal car.

The front suspension is by transverse torsion bars and parallel trailing arms. Patented by Dr Porsche in 1931, this rugged system was also used on the Beetle and pre-war Auto Union Grand Prix car. Both the front and rear brake drums are cast iron Beetle items.

There are many cars which possess good roadholding characteristics and which one can really drive to the limit of adhesion. Once this limit is crossed by just the slightest margin, these cars break loose and with such force that the steering correction will hardly keep them on the road. The Porsche announces the fact that it intends to break loose, a little in advance, by a side wiping of the rear wheels and if one does the correct thing at this particular moment, then the first wiping away of the rear wheels becomes completely harmless. As a matter of fact, you will feel, from prolonged experience, that this is a completely normal and controllable action.'

STEERING

From a driver's point of view, everything about the 356 feels as though it is precision made and the steering is no exception. Light, crisp and direct with two and a half turns from lock to lock, it works by transverse link and unequal length track rods. The steering gearbox itself, a simple worm and nut unit similar to the one used on the Beetle, is clamped to the top of the upper torsion bar tube. A rubber disc interwoven with canvas was fitted between the steering column and the steering box to help reduce vibrations through the steering mechanism from the road. One important modification occurred much later, in September 1958, when a new steering arm was introduced, to correct the difference in the angle of the steering wheel between the full left and full

Transversely mounted torsion bars and trailing arms were also used for the rear suspension and are virtually unbreakable. The shock absorber, here mounted at an angle, was repositioned vertically in 1955. To the right of the brake drum, the rocker box cover shows clearly how neatly the engine fits into the tail.

right lock. As a result, the toe-in was changed from 5.7mm to 1.3mm unloaded, and from 4.5mm to 0.1mm loaded.

BRAKES

Initially, the production Porsches were fitted with hydraulically-operated drum brakes, whereas the prototype had utilised the Volkswagen's cable-operated system. In early 1950, Lockheed hydraulic brakes were adopted. The cast iron drums were 230mm (8.97in) in diameter at front and rear, the brake cylinders were 19mm (0.75in) units, and the shoes were 30mm (1.17in) in width. The braking system was entirely conventional, consisting of two leading shoes at the front and one leading and one trailing shoe at the rear, two return springs, a shoe retainer spring on the top and bottom, shoe anchors and an operating lever. Energit 999 was used for the brake lining material. The handbrake was operated by cables on the rear wheels.

Notoriously inaccessible, the brake fluid reservoir, which was made of tin, was positioned on top of the master cylinder just behind the front torsion bar tubes. In October 1952, Porsche introduced new light alloy drums of 280mm (10.92in) diameter, which at the front were finned radially and went a long way towards increasing overall braking efficiency. At the same time the width of the front shoes was increased to 40mm (1.56in), but the rear shoes remained at 30mm (1.17in).

In November 1953, the *The Autocar*'s road testers were able to write: 'The brakes are in keeping with the performance, the car pulling up straight even with all wheels locked. The pedal pressure required for an emergency stop is fairly heavy, but at no time was any tendency to fade noticed.'

CONCLUSION

By the time of the introduction of the 356A or T1 model at the Frankfurt Motor Show in September 1955, Porsche had already come a very long way. The 356 had been developed in typically German fashion with production modifications (see page 105) carried out only when the engineers had found a better way of doing things.

Customers' views on how the car could be improved were taken into consideration, usually through information fed back through the sales network, but on the whole the company forged a single-minded path of development based on sound engineering principles, and the amount of money that could be spared for research and tooling, not merely to appease the whims of fashion.

On 21 March 1951, Porsche celebrated the production of its 500th sports car. Just five years later, on 16 March 1956, employees proudly grouped themselves around their 10,000th car, a metallic blue 356A coupé. Sales continued to climb but there was always room for improvement and development continued.

THE 356A (1955-59)

The car announced at the Frankfurt Motor Show in September 1955 for the 1956 model year was the much improved 356A, which was updated until the introduction of the 356B, officially announced at the Frankfurt Motor Show in 1959. The 356A was a logical development of the Porsche philosophy, more comfortable, luxurious and responsive, safer and easier to drive than the original Porsche, but nothing in the 356A's specification suggested a break into wholly new territory.

The comprehensive range comprised the coupé, cabriolet and the Speedster, introduced in 1954. Engine choice extended to the 1300 and 1600 in Normal and Super forms and the Carrera 1500 four-cam. Cars fitted with the Normal engines became known as Ladies in Britain, Dames in North America and Damen in Germany because they were generally smoother and more pleasant to drive. The T1

When the 356A was introduced in 1955, it was designated the T1 and the 'Pre-A' cars became known retrospectively as T0. The T1 was much the same as before but many detail changes genuinely improved it.

This superb view of Tim Dawson's 356A clearly shows how the front of the roof line was no longer bent. It was now rounded to accommodate the more modern, curved windscreen.

version of the 356A remained in production until the advent of the T2, announced at the Frankfurt Motor Show in September 1957. Again there were several changes although many of the modifications, such as the attractive teardrop shaped rear lights, had actually been introduced earlier that year in March. So successful was the T2 style that very few changes were made in 1958, the 356A remaining virtually the same in its specification until the launch the

following year of the substantially different 356B.

The Autocar in its 1956 road test wrote of the revised 356: 'The sports racing background to the Porsche is discernible from the moment the car moves off. The driver realises at once that this model is something right out of the run of ordinary cars. The placing of the controls, the seating position, and the acceleration provided by the good power-to-weight ratio, are but part of the first impressions.'

The cabriolet's rear window was enlarged in March 1957 to give improved rear vision, but this superb example is not fitted with door window quarterlights because it was built before September of that year. At some point in 1955 the weave of the cotton hood became finer.

'Teardrop' style rear lights are more usually associated with the T2 introduced in September 1957, but they first appeared, with a number of other revisions, in March.

A perfect Porsche for enjoying in the evening sunshine, this cabriolet, owned by Steve Earl, is painted in one of Porsche's most popular colours – silver metallic. The front number plate is correctly mounted on a bracket.

Praise indeed from a magazine that was restrained even by the standards of 1956. It added: 'To these can be added the high gearing, superb gearchange mechanism, and steering accuracy of the highest order…The model is very much a quality car, assembly of the mechanical components being completed with as much attention to detail as the construction of the Reutter coachwork.'

BODYSHELL & BODY TRIM

Altogether more modern and less austere in appearance than the original Porsche, the 356A is today one of the most desirable in the range, thanks to subtle changes that improved the bodywork. Most obviously, the outer sill panel was flat along its bottom edge, rather than curled under as on the 'Pre-A' cars, and this sill panel was adorned with a protective rubbing strip with a rubber insert. The front and rear wheel arches became considerably more rounded, which can be attributed to the road wheels being reduced from 16in to 15in diameter. The windscreen was now a more conventional and rounded shape, replacing the previous 'bent' item, and so the front scuttle and roof panel were modified accordingly. The new windscreen was not only more aesthetically pleasing as far as most people were concerned, but also offered increased vision.

The chassis frame also underwent a number of modifications during the changeover, not especially significant from a driver's point of view but restorers should be aware of them. The complex inner steel structure was maintained, but some of the sections which make up the frame were altered in shape and size. For example, because the outer body sill panel was straightened out, the jacking point was slightly modified to accommodate it.

The chassis frame behind and in front of the torsion bar tubes was changed when the floor of the nosecone or front panel, which had been a flat panel with a curve along its front edge, became a more angular structure. For some time, the panel under the battery remained flat, as it had been before 1955, but during the early part of 1957 it gained a raised centre section. A towing hook was fitted at the front under the lower nose panel in September 1957. The inner wings and the floor pans remained virtually the same, except that parts of the floorpan were strengthened at strategic points to accept seat belts. The longitudinal members and the heater tubes running through their centres remained unchanged.

At the rear of the chassis frame, the panelwork surrounding the gearbox and pick-up points for the torsion bar tubes was modified when the gearbox was changed to accept two rubber mountings on either side of its nose instead of one. The steel tray around the perimeter of the engine was 'double-stepped' or two-tiered, with the upper tray secured by bolts and the lower one welded to the inside of the bodywork.

The brackets under the front wings which acted

A modified T2 version of the 356A was introduced in September 1957. Although John Hearn's beautifully preserved example looks much the same as the T1 from the front, detail features at the rear include the 'teardrop' style rear lights introduced in March 1957, twin tailpipes routed through the bumper overriders, and the number plate light housing moved from above the number plate to below it.

Compared with sports cars from Britain and Italy, the Porsche's rounded windscreen (right) was slow to arrive. It gave improved panoramic vision and less of a pre-war look. A decorative alloy moulding with a rubber insert (far right) was fitted to each sill on the 356A.

Running the tailpipes through the overriders was a novel idea that helped with ground clearance for that part of the exhaust, although it also meant owners had to clean carbon deposits off the bumpers.

The T2's striker plate was now further down the B-post to accommodate the new position of the door locking mechanism. The hook which secures the rear backrest to a rubber strap can be seen in the background.

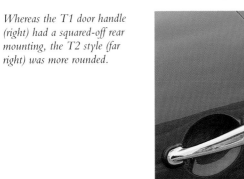

Whereas the T1 door handle (right) had a squared-off rear mounting, the T2 style (far right) was more rounded.

as their strengthening supports, and as a convenient conduit for electrical wiring and a mounting point for the horn, were altered in shape during the early years of the car's development but had become standardised by the time the 356A arrived.

Marked changes to the inner structure of the doors occurred with the introduction of the T2 model in September 1957, when the latches were positioned lower down and the striker plates on the B-posts were moved correspondingly. The door handles were slightly modified in 1957, their rear edges becoming more rounded rather than square.

Chrome-plated bumpers were offered as an option in 1956 but did not really find favour. Incidentally, cars bound for the North American market were fitted with what are today known as 'American-spec' bumpers. At both front and rear, there was an additional tubular bar running above the main blade. However, at some stage during 1957, the tubular bar no longer ran across the full width of the car but was split into two, one each side passing through the overriders and curving downwards into the bumper. The bumpers and lower rear body panel were modified at the rear on the T2 model to include a cut-out for the exhaust system with the tail pipes passing through the bumper overriders (except on the Carrera). This was definitely a backward step: it may have been a convenient way of getting the exhaust pipes out of harm's way, but carbon deposits made a mess of the rear end.

The twin round rear lights soldiered on until March 1957 when they were finally dropped in favour of attractive oval or 'teardrop' lights. As a result, the indicators, tail lights and brake lights were housed behind one lens, the indicator section coloured amber for European models and red for North American ones. A polished bezel surrounding the lens was screwed directly into the bodywork. The registration plate light was now positioned at the bottom of the plate rather than at the top.

Similar to those made for Volkswagen at Wolfsburg, the headlights changed very little over the

years. As an alternative to the Bosch symmetric units, sealed-beam headlights made by Hella were offered which, with their attractive clear lenses, were a popular choice for 356 customers. The front indicators were slightly modified and had the lenses mounted on a chromed pod or housing.

The decorative alloy 'waistline' trim fitted to the Speedster (see page 88) upon its introduction in 1954 and later continued on the Convertible D was absent on coupé and cabriolet models, perhaps because Porsche thought that the 'bathtub' shape of the Speedster needed a strip of trim to break up its appearance, and that mainstream models did not.

It is interesting that automotive engineers who have worked for many years overcoming serious design problems should have devoted so much energy and time to the 356's front lid handle. Originally this item was a perfectly adequate and beautifully-shaped piece of aluminium. In early 1952 it gained a hole at its centre which apparently made lifting the lid easier. In November 1954 the handle became similar to the one fitted to the Speedster two months earlier in September, being longer and incorporating Porsche's stylish enamel crest on its leading edge.

A revised interior (above), which included a newly-introduced perforated vinyl headlining, gave a light, airy feeling to the T1 cabin. This coupé's door cappings and dashboard top should correctly match the interior trim colour. From the start of production cabriolets were supplied with hood bags made of the same material as the top (left). This car's door cappings do match the colour of the interior, but the padded sun visor originally would have been fitted with a vanity mirror.

Incidentally, an interesting story is attached to the crest. Taking a lead from British motor manufacturers who nearly always used some kind of badge proudly displayed on the radiator shells of their cars, Ferry Porsche roughly drew a shield on a paper napkin over lunch with Max Hoffman, the well-known American importer of Porsche cars. Porsche's sketch represented the crest of the House of Wurttemburg, the horse which had long been the City of Stuttgart's

INTERIOR TRIM

Most noticeably, the interior of the 356A was brighter with an altogether more modern feel, largely because the cloth headlining of the previous model was changed for vinyl which extended to cover all the roof pillars. The new headlining had a white finish with a decorative pattern of small dots or perforations.

Adding to the more modern look, the elegant tinted perspex sun visors of the early cars were changed in March 1957 for vinyl-covered, padded items. The Hella interior light was initially unchanged, but for T2 coupés there were two new oval lights, one above each door; cabriolets continued with a single light.

The seats of the cabriolets were nearly always covered in leather, the coupés in vinyl with leather as an extra-cost option. There was a choice of five colours: brown, beige, green, black or red. Generally, the seat material was also used for the interior panels, but a coupé could be ordered with leather for the seats only or for the interior trim panels as well. For restoration purposes, full leather, full vinyl, or leather seats with matching vinyl interior panels are

Thinner seat backrests (above) for the T2 slightly improved rear legroom and the front cushions were reshaped to give better thigh support. This car's door cappings and dashboard top correctly match the interior colour. The chromed door pull at the top of the door panel (right) was moved to a more central position on the T2 version, and the door capping was now trimmed rather than painted.

coat of arms, and the Porsche name as the finishing touch. The authorities in Stuttgart, presented with a proper drawing, gave it their blessing and it has appeared on Porsche cars ever since. The appearance of the Porsche script did not change, except in the number of rivets which fixed it in place, until the advent of the 356B in 1959. Coupés and cabriolets had aluminium alloy scripts front and rear, but those fitted to the Speedster were in brass.

all correct and perfectly acceptable permutations. The rear seats on the coupé were upholstered whereas the cabriolet had carpeting in the rear compartment. Full-width door pockets continued to be featured on all models except the Speedster.

The seats were modified on the T2 in September 1957, becoming more shapely and sporting. The backrests were thinner and the cushions sat higher at the front to give more thigh support. This led to greater comfort and offered more lateral support for hard cornering, welcome improvements for both drivers and front seat passengers.

Reclining front seats were optional from April 1952 but became standard with the introduction of the 356A. Head restraints were offered as optional extras at around the same time. Usually cylindrical in shape and beautifully made, they were attached to the backrests with straps and small clamps, but because the backrests were low and the head restraints were elegantly perched on the top of each seat, it is not easy to see their practical value. But perhaps they were more in the nature of a head 'rest', to be used for those rare moments when Porsche owners stopped at the side of the road on a long continental journey for 40 winks.

The interior door handles and window winders were initially unchanged from the late 'Pre-A' versions, but in September 1957, with the introduction of the T2, the door handles became more rounded, and the window winders became higher geared for easier operation. Few 356 owners will lose sleep over the difficulty of obtaining the correct jacket hooks for their cars, but the prominent alloy hooks screwed to the roof at the top of each 'B' post on the early cars were changed for less stylish, but safer, plastic items in March 1957. Coloured beige, they were still at the top of the 'B' posts but were less hooked in shape. Another minor modification was to the rear view mirror: it had a single-bolt fixing from the start of the 356A, and the attaching bracket was changed from alloy to steel when the T2 was introduced.

For music lovers the 356A was particularly good news because a radio speaker was installed in each of the two 'kick panels', the vertical parts of the front inner wings to the left and right of the front footwells. Very neatly installed, each speaker was surrounded by carpeting and finished with a chrome-plated ring around its perimeter. This arrangement was a great improvement over the old single dash-mounted speaker, which had sounded somewhat 'tinny' by comparison.

Similar hard-wearing carpets were fitted to both the 356 and 356A. These were usually tan or beige, irrespective of colour of the upholstery, and were held in place with a combination of glue and screws. Replacement carpets are readily available these days but it is worth checking the style of the weaving if you wish to achieve 100 per cent authenticity. Rub-

Padded sun visors suitable for a more safety conscious age were introduced in March 1957, replacing the elegant tinted perspex items.

The gear lever on the T2 version was moved slightly back and the heater control knob was moved forward. Rubber mats originally would have been fitted on the floorpan in place of the carpets used on most 356s these days.

ber mats continued to be used on the floor and over the tunnel; those in the 'Pre-A' cars can be distinguished by their ribbed pattern whereas the 356A had a moulded 'pebble-dash' effect.

INSTRUMENTS & CONTROLS

The early cars had a detachable dashboard, but the 356A's was welded into place and its appearance was more modern and sporting. The coupé and cabriolet had the same dashboard whereas the one fitted to the Speedster (see page 88) was altogether different.

The dash panel on the 'Pre-A' cars had had something of a 'juke-box' look about it, with the 'hump' in the middle, but now it was neater and simpler. The upper surface was padded and upholstered rather than painted metal as before, and the ashtray with its 'pull-out, push-in' lid, mounted directly above the radio in the centre, was painted the same colour as the dashboard. From 1957, the ashtray was repositioned at the bottom and was chrome-plated. The elegantly shaped glovebox lid gained a lock in the centre of the chrome-plated knob in early 1956. The passenger grab handle, a plastic one from the Beetle on 'Pre-A' cars, was now chromed.

The three main instruments had black faces with green lettering as before but they were now the same size, and the glass was flat rather than dished and a little closer to the face. Naturally, speedometers differed according to the country for which the cars

No longer detachable, the T1's modernised dashboard looked superb. The three main instruments were equal in size with integral warning lights, the upper surface of the dash panel was padded (and originally colour-matched to the upholstery), and the shapely glovebox lid acquired a chromed lock. This car is fitted with a Derrington wood-rim steering wheel, a common contemporary accessory on UK cars. A more modern radio (right) became available, with twin speakers positioned in the side kick panels. The ashtray, which moved below the radio on the later T2 cars, has a Hella light above it.

were destined: those for Britain and North America were calibrated to 120mph and those for the European market to 200kph, except for Carrera versions (see page 72). All the instruments were generally VDO units (replacing Veigel), finished with a chromed outer bezel and incorporating the various warning lights which, on the 'Pre-A' series, had been placed separately on the dashboard.

At first the 356A had its instruments arranged with the tachometer in the middle, the speedometer on the left and the combined oil temperature and fuel gauge on the right, but on the introduction of

the T2 the outer dials swapped places. This arrangement sufficed for both left- and right-hand drive. The mechanically-driven 6000rpm tachometer was red-lined at 4500rpm on 1300 and 1600 (Normal) models or 5000rpm on 1300S and 1600S (Super) versions. A small, manually adjusted clock was optional for the 356A and could be fitted to the lid of the glovebox. An electrically operated clock positioned in the middle of the dash panel was introduced for the T2 as standard.

Whereas the 'Pre-A' cars had a separate ignition switch and starter button, the 356A was fitted with a combined ignition/starter switch, located to the left of the instruments on coupés and cabriolets but to the right on the Speedster. When the updated T2 was announced, the centre part of the ignition/starter switch, into which the key fits, was slightly enlarged. A cigarette lighter was standard (except on the Speedster), and positioned to the left of the radio. As with the late 'Pre-A' cars, the dashboard knobs and switchgear were available in three colours – ivory, grey or beige – to match the steering wheel.

One of the most obvious changes to the 356A was that the steering wheel gained a full circle horn ring to replace the old segmented item that had been introduced in late 1954, and the plastic-rimmed wheel initially came in a choice of sizes – 400mm (15.75in) or 425mm (16.75in) – although the larger size became standard for the T2 version with the new ZF steering box (see page 48). Although the

horn ring had practical value, allowing the driver to sound the horn with his hand anywhere on the wheel, it was far from pretty and somewhat out of keeping with the car's sporting image. By this time, though, the road cars were beginning to appeal to a much wider audience. The 356 was a comfortable, safe and practical vehicle, and for those with more sporting aspirations there were alternative steering wheels that could be specified.

The factory-fitted steering wheels from VDM and Nardi each had three alloy spokes and a wood rim, but are rarely seen. Both were extra-cost options. These wheels differed in detail, however, because VDM used a Porsche horn button whereas Nardi used its own type, but both displayed the Porsche crest. Some Nardi steering wheels were fitted with a horn ring which also doubled as a headlamp flasher. These attractive but expensive steering wheels are similar to the wood-rimmed wheels supplied by Derrington for the British market. For anyone wanting to upgrade their cars today, the Moto-Lita steering wheels ape the 1950s style exceptionally well and are less expensive than original wheels.

The handbrake was no longer fitted with a conventional ratchet, but became an 'in-out' affair operated with a twisting action. It had a chromed handle and was not now attached to the steering column. However, a conventional handbrake on the floor might have been more satisfactory for rally drivers who relished the thought of a fast handbrake turn on tight hairpin bends.

A more satisfactory pedal cluster was instituted on the 356A. The pedals were still hinged at the bottom, of course, but the brake and clutch pedal arms, which had been in one piece, became jointed roughly in the middle so that they could be adjusted for reach. The cluster was also removable, making servicing a little easier. Whereas the pedal pads on 'Pre-A' cars were roughly rectangular in shape, on the 356A they became 'rectilinear', curving in towards the bottom on both sides. A hand throttle was an addition and was operated by a knob near the bottom of the dashboard, close to the instruments. A novel idea, the hand throttle was a substitute for the choke, but it was dropped for the 356B.

The floor-mounted heater control knob continued to be positioned between the seats behind the gear lever on the T1, but moved slightly forward of the lever on the T2. The Porsche's heating system was extremely effective until rust took its toll on the exhaust system, when fumes could find their way into the cabin with the heat. However, it is perfectly serviceable provided that it is kept in good condition. In its road test of October 1958, the The Autocar remarked: 'The various heater-ventilator controls, in combination with the trailing quarter windows, make it possible to control the interior temperature over a very wide range, and there are no traces of fumes when the heater is working.'

Porsche achieved an altogether more satisfactory package with the 356A. More modern, ergonomically superior to the old model, with greatly

The T2's dashboard remained much the same, but an optional electric clock could now be fitted above the radio and the ashtray was positioned below it. The standard two-spoke steering wheel gained a full horn ring, as seen here, on all 356A models.

The road wheels were reduced in diameter from 16in to 15in and increased in width from 3.25in to 4.5in, a particularly welcome modification. The standard tyres were 5.60 × 15 crossplies but more modern radials are fitted here. The five wheel studs can be seen with the hubcap removed. A customer could specify wheels in body colour, although the usual finish was silver paint or chrome.

limit of adhesion offered by the skinny crossply tyres. At just 3.25in wide the rims and track were so narrow that resulting body 'overhang' made the cars look rather awkward. With the introduction of the new model, Porsche reduced the diameter of the wheels to 15in and increased their width to 4.5in, which was a most welcome improvement.

At the same time, the tyre size was changed from 5.00 × 16 to 5.60 × 15 but, as before, they were crossplies. Radials were still being developed in the mid-1950s and even after companies like Pirelli started making them in the early 1960s for general sale, the majority of the world's car manufacturers continued to offer the much cheaper crossply rubber. Porsche, however, was comparatively quick to cotton on to the advantages of radial tyres and later offered them on the 356B.

The design of the road wheel itself did not change and was to the same five-stud Porsche pattern, with 10 ventilation holes which aided brake cooling and helped to reduce unsprung weight. The wheels on most cars were finished in silver paint or chrome, but some were painted to match the body colour, an aesthetically interesting exercise although not strictly in keeping with the more modern appearance Porsche was seeking. Attractive chrome-plated hubcaps, which by this time were known as 'baby moons', were still fitted to the 15in wheels, and the Porsche crest which featured at their centres from September 1957 was standard on the Super version but optional on the Damen.

Special wheels were available for the Carrera GT which had alloy rims and steel centres. As an alternative, the attractively styled Rudge 'knock-off' racing wheels were an option, but could not be fitted to the 356's standard brake drums.

improved forward visibility, and a little more comfortable, it was a huge success in all markets where it was sold. Sales figures began to rise and journalists offered virtually no criticism of the cockpit. Indeed *The Autocar* commented in October 1958: 'The Reutter seats are outstandingly good, the backrests being adjustable from the vertical almost to the prone position; upholstery is comfortable yet firm and gives ample support to the back and shoulders as well as the thighs; the seats also locate the occupants laterally. With variable rake of the backrests, the fore-and-aft adjustment of the seats (which is considerable) and the variation of reach available even on the pedal pads themselves, it is possible to set the driving position to suit anyone. Upholstery is in good quality leathercloth, with floor coverings in rubber; a form of carpeting is used to cover the interior of the body sides.'

These comments still hold true today. Merely sitting in one of these fine cars gives a good insight into what the small team at Porsche had achieved through genuine improvement. Nothing had been changed for the sake of it and to many the 356A was a much better car than the original 356, but understandably out-and-out purists will disagree.

WHEELS & TYRES

The narrow 16in diameter wheels fitted to the early 356 Porsches were considered adequate for their day, except of course by those who had overstepped the

ELECTRICS

The electrical system was still fired by a six-volt, 84Ah battery. However, Porsche did change the battery cover from alloy to fibreboard shortly after the 356A was introduced. In typically restrained fashion, *The Autocar* said: 'More powerful headlights would be desirable for drivers intending to use the full speed of the car at night.' One English journalist even praised the power of the 356A's headlamps, but one can only assume that he had had a hectic road test schedule and got his notes mixed up with those for another car. The headlamps were still fitted with 35 watt bulbs for high and low beams.

The Bosch spark plugs continued as before with the 1300 and 1600 Normal models having the W22T1 variety and the 1300S and 1600S cars getting W240T1 items. From 1957, Champion L10S or Beru 225-14 became additional choices for the 1600, and Champion 111S or Beru 240-14 for the 1600S. The distributor, starter motor and plug leads

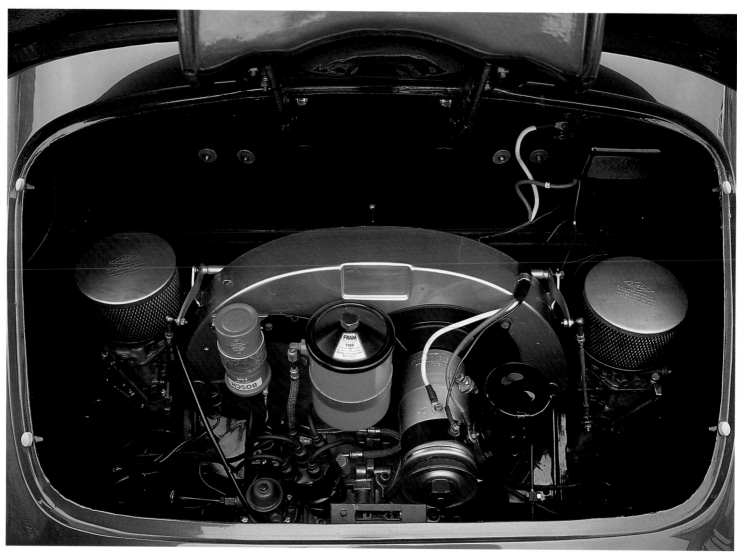

remained much the same. However, cars with a two-piece crankcase can be distinguished by a flat-topped distributor cap. The later cars with a three-piece crankcase have a distributor with a domed cap.

ENGINE

The most important change for the new model was an increase in size for the larger engine, from 1500 to 1600, giving four basic engine options: 1300, 1300S, 1600 and 1600S. The stroke of the new engine remained at 74mm (2.89in), the same as in the 1300 and 1500 engines, but the bore was increased to 82.5mm (3.22in) to give an overall size of 1582cc (96.50cu in). There were two types of 1600 engine: the Normal version with the plain-bearing crankshaft which developed a maximum 60bhp at 4500rpm with a compression ratio of 7.5:1, and the Super with the roller-bearing crankshaft which pushed out a healthy 75bhp at 5000rpm with a higher compression ratio at 8.5:1.

Both versions of the 1300 engine continued in

Normal (1286cc, 80 × 64mm) and Super (1290cc, 74.5 × 74mm) forms with a choice of 44bhp or 60bhp, the Super developing the same power as the 1600 Normal model. The difference between the roller-bearing 1300S and the 1600 engine with the plain-bearing crankshaft, however, was the way in which each power unit reached its maximum output. The 1300S's maximum power was achieved at 5500rpm and the 1600's at 4500rpm, so less effort was required from the driver with the larger-engined car. At the end of 1957, the 1300 engines were dropped from the range.

Naturally, the new 1600 power units were welcomed by those who could afford the relatively high price. It is interesting to realise that although the new cars were capable of relatively high speeds – in excess of 100mph – the specific output per litre at 38bhp (Normal) and 47.4bhp (Super) was still not very great. But the real advantage that singled out the 356 from many other fast cars was that it was totally reliable for thousands of miles, and tractable at the same time. It could be driven to the centre of any

Apart from the Carrera four-cam introduced in 1955, there were 1300 and 1600 engines, both in Normal and Super guises. Silver-grey fan housings, as on this 1600S, were reserved for Supers. The blue Bosch coil, although not original, is the convenient modern fitment.

During the 1950s 'cooking' Porsches – this is a 1600 – were known as Damen in Germany, Dames in North America and Ladies in Britain because of their sweet, easy-going nature, and are distinguished by their black painted fan housings.

large city for a shopping trip without the plugs oiling up or the engine overheating, something which could not truthfully be claimed for the Ferraris and Maseratis of the period.

The new engine produced maximum torque of 80lb ft at 2800rpm in the 1600 version or 85lb ft at 3700rpm for the 1600S, such was the difference between plain and roller-bearing crankshafts. Twin Solex 32PBJ carburettors were used in both cases. Typically, the 1600S could be expected to reach 0-60mph in around 15sec and a top speed of approximately 103mph, while returning 30mpg in normal driving conditions. Both the Damen and Super versions were fitted with twin tail pipes from September 1957. At the same time, the heater boxes were fitted with pre-heater pipes leading to the carburettors to aid cold starting.

From September 1958, some small modifications were made to the engine. The Super version was fitted with a plain-bearing crankshaft because the roller-bearing unit, although it gave greater, smoother performance, wore out rather quickly and

rebuilds were complex and expensive. At the same time, the Damen or Normal version was fitted with iron cylinder barrels instead of aluminium-alloy, a change which went a long way to quietening the air-cooled engine. To distinguish between the two, the 75bhp unit was given a silver fan housing, whereas the Normal versions were still black. New twin-choke Zenith 32 NDIX carburettors gave smoother engine running, and to improve the oil pressure at low running speeds and generally increase oil circulation the crankcase's oilways were reworked. A stronger oil cooler was installed to cope with increased oil pressure and, for the first time, the engine was fitted with an 'oilstat' or thermostat which controlled the oil temperature automatically and efficiently – critical with an air-cooled engine because the oil contributes to heat dissipation.

Up to the introduction of the 356B in 1959, Porsche concentrated most of its development efforts in areas other than the engine, and the bodywork, creature comforts and the chassis all came in for detail attention. Because the 1100 engine had been discarded in 1954 and the 1300 power unit in 1957, it is obvious that customers were voting with their pockets for the more powerful cars. Slowly but surely the company started to go 'up market', and by the late 1950s it had started to work on a total replacement for the 356, Porsche having realised quickly that it must now satisfy the demands of a more affluent society.

TRANSMISSION

The 356A continued to be fitted with the traditional Porsche synchromesh gearbox, the casing of which was split vertically and longitudinally, but it was mounted differently. Instead of having just one rubber mounting on its 'nose', two were fitted either side of the nose. This type of gearbox is known as the dual-mount 519. The new mounts were made of stiffer rubber and helped to minimise vibrations and stress imposed on the transmission by the engine and suspension.

From September 1957, the 356A was fitted with a new one-piece gearbox, commonly referred to as transmission 644 or the tunnel-case gearbox. Like its predecessor it was a neat and compact unit, and was ribbed for strength and additional cooling. An improved synchronising mechanism was added in 1958 with an additional oil seal for the gear linkage in the front cover, and this later gearbox carries the serial number 716.

The Autocar, in its test of the 1600 in October 1958, remarked on the complete absence of transmission noise but commented: 'The gear change is smooth, and the lever easily reached, but it requires a fairly long movement: the synchromesh is good, though it is possible to override it in snap changes upwards from first to second.' There were several other differences between the two types of gearbox, but all of a highly technical nature, and really Porsche gearboxes are best left to the experts.

The new gear ratios were as follows: first 3.182:1, second 1.765:1, third 1.130:1, fourth 0.815:1 and reverse 3.56:1. These figures apply to the 1300, 1600 and 1600S in both coupé and cabriolet forms. A new diaphragm clutch, still 180mm (7.02in) in size, was introduced with the T2 in September 1957, and had the effect of increasing the pressure at the clutch plate while reducing pedal pressure by as much as 75 per cent, allowing greater torque to be transmitted without the clutch plate slipping. At the same time as these significant transmission changes were made, the gear lever was shortened.

SUSPENSION

From September 1955, the 356A was equipped with vertically mounted telescopic shock absorbers at the rear, replacing the angled ones of the 'Pre-A'. At the same time, the springing was softened to improve ride quality and the suspension travel was increased. Nonetheless, the suspension system remained as unbreakable as ever, although purists bemoaned the soggier feel under hard cornering.

STEERING

An important change saw the 356A fitted with a hydraulic telescopic steering damper, which was connected between the drop arm and a small clamp around the lower of the two front axle tubes. This had the effect of minimising or even negating liveliness in the steering. It is difficult to appreciate the importance of this small but vital component until a worn one makes its presence felt by feeding every jolt and bump through the steering wheel.

In September 1957, Porsche took the opportunity to replace the Volkswagen steering box with one made by ZF. A worm and peg affair, the worm was carried on ball bearings and had a splined joint connected to a flexible joint which was joined to the steering column. A criticism of the Volkswagen steering box was that it had too much free play and was a little sloppy. The ZF unit was bigger, had a four-stud fixing instead of two and a greater range of adjustment giving more precision. The king pins still needed greasing every 1500 miles, the steering angles and toe-in required checking every 3000 miles, and the SAE 90 steering gearbox oil needed topping up at 6000 mile intervals, but regular maintenance has always been the key to a mechanically healthy 356.

BRAKES

Drum diameter continued to be 280mm (10.92in) on the 356A, but the width of the rear brake shoes increased to 40mm (1.56in), the same size as the front shoes. For restoration purposes, the internal diameter wear limit of the drums is 282mm – drums can be machined if they have worn or 'ovalled' within this limit.

CONCLUSION

The 356A was the perfect sports car for its time. When production ended, 21,045 356As had been sold. The Suez oil crisis of 1956 made no difference to Porsche's customers, but the strides made by other manufacturers did. Cars became more extravagantly designed, particularly in the important American market, and Porsche had little option but to keep up with developments. Not that its philosophy on sports cars changed: while manufacturers from Italy and Britain brought out completely new models, Porsche merely updated the existing one and announced the 356B in 1959.

The fastest of the 356A models was the 1600 Super, fitted with a roller-bearing crankshaft at first but a plain-bearing one (in the interests of durability) after September 1958.

THE 356B (1959-63)

THE 356B

After a period of relatively few changes through 1957 and 1958, the 'facelifted' 356B T5 was introduced in September 1959. The car's appearance was substantially altered by the higher mounting of the bumpers and headlamps. Although this new look was not to everyone's taste, sales increased significantly.

Throughout 1958, Ferry Porsche and his team were working on ideas to update the 356 and a number of schemes were mooted, both for the revised car and the future. The company had carried out some market research to discover exactly what its customers required, and the results brought about some changes, although Porsche refused to compromise quality, engineering integrity or its reputation for making sporting cars. Design studies for a T3 and T4 version were shelved before the end of 1958. It is interesting that the T4 study included twin headlamps but the upper echelons of the company's management team did not consider that their customers were ready for such radical innovations.

The differences between the 356A and the first T5 version of the 356B were much more radical than those between the original car and the 356A, although externally they still appeared similar. Changes were made in nearly all parts of the car, and the great majority proved to be improvements. There were further bodyshell changes for the T6 version in 1961. However, when the revised 356B was launched at the Frankfurt Motor Show in

September 1959, it received a mixed reaction.

Some purists could not accept the altered styling, thinking it made the car look heavier, flabbier and less nimble. At this time, Porsche even considered the possibility of using air suspension, and even of producing a four-seater version of the 356, which would have been a brave move for a company that had hitherto only produced sporting two-seaters. Both ideas were shelved, and the company's hunch that a four-seater might then have damaged its reputation was probably right. The 356B range consisted of a Coupé, Cabriolet and Roadster (see page 97), the latter replacing the Convertible D of the late A-series. The odd looking Karmann Hardtop was introduced for the 1961 model year. Carrera versions continued as usual (see page 72).

Soon after the 356B went into production, it developed a number of small problems which required urgent attention. The change from cast iron rocker arms to alloy, with a corresponding modification in the rocker arm ratio, which was intended to improve the car's acceleration, turned out to be a backward step. The new car was slower, and so

Porsche reverted to the original specification. Later, the gear linkage mechanism was found to be defective and modifications had to be made to the new, 'improved' mountings.

Despite these initial problems, the 356B was a better car than its predecessors. Higher performance was available from the new Super 90 model, and improvements to the chassis did much to curtail the car's tendency to oversteer. It remained one of the world's most reliable sports cars with the usual excellent build quality.

Porsche continued to develop the 356B with the aim of producing an even better car. Although journalists had almost stopped complaining about the car's supposed disadvantages, even beginning to look upon it as an old friend, the company took this potentially dangerous view seriously and worked flat out in its seemingly never-ending quest for the ultimate 356. Good old friends are nice to have but most customers are always looking to meet new and more exciting ones.

BODYSHELL & BODY TRIM

One of the reasons why motoring enthusiasts regard cars made during the 1950s and 1960s as classics is that they often seem to have more character. With their round headlamps, metal bumpers and curving bonnets, many had 'faces' with which the car buying public could identify, and the 356 was no exception. It had a happy countenance that greeted its owner with a reassuring smile. But while the 356A had looked purposeful, ready to get on with a day's hard motoring, the 356B had a superior look which almost bordered on impudence.

The T5 body, in many ways similar to the 356A, had many subtle changes in detail which meant that some of the panels were not interchangeable with the earlier model. The front wings adopted a different profile to accommodate the headlights, now mounted a little higher and at a more vertical angle. The front lid was contoured more sharply at the

The final incarnation of the 356 bodyshell appeared in the T6 version of the 356B in 1961. Two air intakes sat side by side on the rear lid, to replace the traditional single intake, the cabriolet's hood acquired an opening (and larger) rear window, and coupés had their windscreens and back windows enlarged.

This overhead shot illustrates how the 356's appearance – its body curves and overall stance – had changed from the slim and austere cars of the early 1950s to the sophisticated, middle-aged Bs and Cs of the 1960s.

front, an arguable improvement, and the nose panel was more steeply raked. The front scuttle and window area were left unmodified but quarterlights (not seen as standard since the Gmünd cars) were built into the door windows.

Now heavier, stronger and bigger, the bumpers were mounted higher, by 95mm (3.7in) at the front and 105mm (4.1in) at the rear, and were fitted with much larger and more effective overriders whose appearance did not always find favour. The rear overriders continued to have cut-outs for the exhaust tail pipes, and two number plate lights were built into the bumper. As a result of the rear bumper change, the tail lights had to be moved further up the rear panel.

The horn grilles now had two alloy slats and were slightly narrower than before. Below the bumper was a small grille on each side to improve ventilation to the brakes. For some reason, Porsche could not resist altering the front lid handle again and made it broader at the front, giving the car an almost human-

looking nose to complement the large 'eyes' suggested by the headlamps. As before, the Porsche crest was mounted on the front of the handle. The indicators were altered slightly in shape, with amber lenses for the European and British markets and clear lenses for cars sold in North America.

The existing style of lettering continued to be used for the front and rear Porsche scripts but they were roughly a couple of centimetres wider, and there were additional gold-coloured badges to denote the different models: 1600, 1600 Super and Super 90 (or just a '90' badge on T6 versions). After 1960, most cars were without a script on the front panel. Below the doors, the trim applied to each sill, including the rubber insert, was slightly narrower and more elegant.

Most of the sheet metalwork that formed the structure of the chassis frame remained unaltered on the 356B, and certainly major alterations were unnecessary. However, the strengthening brackets under the front wings that acted as a convenient

The headlamps of the T5 were mounted higher, which necessitated a slight modification to the shape of the wings. The horn grille now has two horizontal slats instead of three, the bumper is 95mm higher and the indicators sit on larger bases. The front lid handle has changed shape again but is still fitted with the Porsche crest.

point on which to mount the horn, and as a conduit for the headlamp wiring, were slightly altered in shape because of the 'facelifted' bodywork. The floorpan was altered to accommodate the different gearchange rod and linkage made necessary when the gearbox nose was initially fitted with a single rubber mounting. At the rear, the pan and rear cross pieces were altered to accommodate revised seats.

After only two years, Porsche made further changes to the 356's appearance when the T6 version appeared. To some, it resembled a frog or a turtle on four wheels. To others, its beauty was without rival. The nose was modified again: the front lid was wider at the front and instead of being curved along its front edge, the line was flatter, giving the car a shovel-like appearance. On left-hand drive cars access to the fuel filler neck became easier when it was transferred to the outside of the right-hand front wing, removing the need to open the bonnet when filling up. The front bulkhead was also altered to suit. This could not be done on right-hand drive cars because the steering column and other components would have blocked the route of the pipe from the filler to the fuel tank. Fresh air was admitted to the cabin through a bank of 28 louvres cut into the scuttle in front of the windscreen, although not on the Roadster version.

The windscreen and the rear window on the T6 were both increased in size, and the decorative aluminium alloy trims around their perimeters were made slightly wider, helping to create the impression that the 356 was becoming just a little heavier in its middle age. For the T6, the optional sunroof was electrically operated, manual operation being

Although optional on coupés since 1957 and standard on GT Carreras, window quarterlights (left), not otherwise seen on coupés since the Gmünd period, made a welcome return as standard on the 356B. The higher bumpers and larger overriders (below) were accompanied by two small registration plate lights fitted to the top of the bumper to replace the housing previously attached to the bodywork.

The lower A-post is fitted with a switch to operate the interior light, and carries two aluminium plates, the upper one giving the name of the coachbuilder and chassis number, the lower one the body paint code number.

When the 90bhp 1600 debuted in 1959, it was badged in gold-coloured script as a 'Super 90'. By the time the T6 appeared, the 'Super' had been dropped and the car was simply badged as a '90'.

With its sandwich filling of horsehair, the fully-lined hood was as beautifully constructed as ever, although some owners experienced difficulties in sealing the top to the side windows. An innovatory zip (far right) in the cabriolet's hood allowed the rear window to be removed, enabling the driver and passenger to enjoy fresh air without taking the top down.

With its larger glass area and improved all-round visibility, the Karmann Hardtop introduced in 1960 should have been a success, but its 'notchback' appearance was not popular – and surviving specimens are very rare today. This model is not to be confused with the removable hardtop offered to cabriolet owners from 1958.

dropped altogether. The shapely engine lid was also increased in size, allowing better access, and it now had 'twin banked' intakes of the same size sitting side by side. Before the T6, standard road cars always had a single bank of louvres in the centre of the engine lid, only the GT Carrera versions introduced in 1956 having two banks of six louvres on either side of the central intake. The aluminium grilles which slotted into place inside the engine lid apertures were also slightly changed, the thin cross pieces of the mesh becoming tubular instead of flat.

Under the bonnet of left-hand drive T6 models was a new, flatter fuel tank but still with a capacity of 57 litres, although a 70-litre tank was an option. The luggage compartment was fitted with a plastic liner, the spare wheel was mounted more horizontally, the fusebox with its new fibreboard cover was moved behind the dashboard and the battery was relocated on the right. Right-hand drive cars retained the older style T5 fuel tank with a capacity of 57 litres.

A hardtop coupé version launched in 1960 was built by Karmann on the cabriolet bodyshell, the hardtop being firmly welded into place. With its dis-

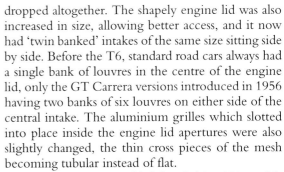

Individual rear seats fitted with folding backrests allowed the cushions to be mounted lower, increasing the available headroom. The rear window sill was originally painted in a similar colour to the interior trim, not in the body colour.

tinctive 'notchback' styling, this model should not be confused with the cabriolet itself, which could be fitted with a detachable hardtop. The idea behind the project was to widen the 356's appeal and some people appreciated the increase in all-round visibility created by the longer rear and side windows. The Karmann production hardtop cars can generally be distinguished from the cabriolets fitted with detachable hardtops by their paintwork, which was usually all in one colour, whereas a separate hardtop would have been in different colour from the body. A sunroof was available as an extra-cost option on the Karmann hardtop. When the T6 body was introduced in 1961, the Karmann hardtop gained a grooved ridge along the front edge of the roof, but poor sales led to the model being dropped a year later.

INTERIOR TRIM

The interior changed very little on the introduction of the 356B. The rear seats on the T5 were split into two with folding backrests which allowed the base of the seats to be situated nearer the floorpan, increasing the headroom by 60mm (2.34in). For the T6, the runners on which the front seats were mounted were strengthened and the reclining seats gained a safety locking mechanism. The upholstery for all 356Bs was unchanged and the available colours were black, red, light grey, dark grey, blue or brown.

As an extra-cost option, customers could specify

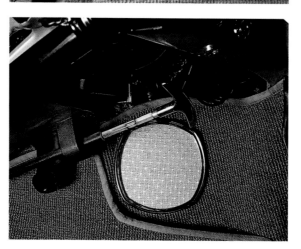

Perhaps incongruous in a sports car, the push-pull handbrake lever had a chromed handle (left) until it was changed for one with a dull finish upon the introduction of the T6 in 1961 (below left). Factory-fitted loudspeaker grilles were placed in the front side kick panels, and became smaller when the 356C was introduced.

A new 'tulip' shaped dished safety steering wheel (a horn ring was now optional) and black plastic dashboard knobs distinguished the T5 from its predecessors. The cluster gauge and speedometer had swapped places on the introduction of the T2 in 1957, and remained in the same position until the end of production. An electrically-operated clock (right) was fitted as standard to the 356B, its winder moving from the bottom of the face to the centre with the introduction of the T6.

the seat squabs and backrests with perforations. All cabriolets had leather upholstery and trim as standard but, strangely, vinyl was offered as an alternative. As before, the headlining was in cream vinyl with perforations or dots. The window winders and door handles remained unchanged but the knobs, escutcheons and dashboard knobs and buttons were all in black plastic. The rear view mirror also remained unchanged and carpeting was in the familiar coarse-weave cloth.

The larger windscreen on the T6 transformed the whole character of the cabin. It became lighter and more spacious, with greatly improved visibility. Making a break with the snug, 'protective' interiors of past years, it reflected a new age – the 1960s.

INSTRUMENTS & CONTROLS

The dashboard remained the same on the 356B except that the various knobs and switches were now in black and an electric clock was fitted as standard in the centre of the panel. The clock was adjustable with a small winder, which was moved from the bottom of the clock to the centre when the T6 was introduced. The gear lever on the T6 was shortened and was chrome-plated instead of having a painted finish in silver.

Fresh air vents were introduced on the centre of the scuttle in front of the windscreen of the T6 and a new lever in the centre of the dash controlled the flow of air to the cabin. In cars fitted with an optional heater fan (introduced on the 356B), there was an additional lever to control it. In an era before electrically heated rear windows became commonplace, the 356B coupé was fitted with additional demisting ducts to the back window. The heater ducts in the sills now took the form of an aluminium alloy slide, which could be moved fore and aft to control the flow of warm air.

A single stalk mounted on the left-hand side of steering column continued to operate both the headlamp flasher unit and the indicators, but it was longer, more angular and flatter, losing some of the elegance of the previous slim item. The stalk was on the right-hand side on right-hand drive cars.

From the start of the 356B the steering wheel became a dished three-spoke item with a black plastic rim and polished alloy spokes. The horn ring disappeared except as an optional extra, which seems to have been rarely requested. The twist-and-pull handbrake remained the same except that its finish was matt instead of bright on the T6.

WHEELS & TYRES

The familiar five-stud 15in ventilated steel wheels of 15in diameter and 4½in width were fitted to the 356B, with both rims and centres painted silver. Fitted to the wheels with spring clips, the hubcaps were unchanged, and the attractive Porsche crest came as standard on the Super, Super 90 and Carrera models, and as an option on the Damen 356.

A very important change for the 356B, however, concerned the tyres, because at long last various tyre companies had found an alternative to the old unsatisfactory crossply tyres. Radial-ply tyres were now perfected and Porsche was quick to offer them as standard equipment on the 356B, a change that contributed greatly to driving enjoyment. Michelin, Continental and Dunlop tyres were favoured and the standard size was 165 × 15in front and rear. Some enthusiastic owners, though, claimed that the handling could be further enhanced by fitting 155s at the front, making it easier to 'pivot' the front in a tight bend while sliding the rear.

For today's owners, 165 × 15 radials not only have superior durability and roadholding qualities but are also still readily and cheaply available. Michelins are the preferred choice for many owners despite their higher price, but the original 'X' pattern is virtually unobtainable today.

ELECTRICS

The fusebox and battery were moved on the T6 model. In the case of the battery, this was simply because the shape of the front end of the car had been modified, and also led to the braided earth strap being shortened. A Bosch six-volt 84Ah battery was standard, but a 12-volt 50Ah battery was available to special order. As usual, there was a choice of sparking plugs, between Beru D225/14, Champion L85 and Bosch W225 T7.

The T6 was treated to a more efficient 50 watt variable speed windscreen wiper motor which was operated by turning a knob on the wiper switch on the dashboard, but this more sophisticated item does tend to give more trouble than the simpler one-speed motor. Rattles and vibrations in the windscreen wiper blades are quite common, but they can usually be cured by fiddling with the rubber washers that fit over the wiper arm cranks. The headlights, which were the same as those employed on the Bee-

tle, remained unchanged and took the form of the standard left-hand drive Bosch items, asymmetric units for right-hand drive cars or optional sealed beam lights. For cars fitted with the regular 6-volt electrical system, the headlamp bulbs were uprated to 45/40 watts, and the indicator lamps and brake lights were increased from 15 to 18 watts. The corresponding lamps fitted to the optional 12-volt system were rated the same as the 6-volt cars. Neither the 6-volt nor 12-volt cars were uprated when the 356C was introduced. An electrically operated sunroof (instead of manual) was offered as an extra-cost option on the T6.

ENGINE

The 1600 and 1600S pushrod engines remained unaltered and continued to develop 60bhp at 4500rpm and 75bhp at 5000rpm respectively. In addition there was the new Super 90 – so called because it developed 90bhp – which still used pushrods to operate the valvegear. The new engine, code number 616/7, was a reworked version of the 1600 75bhp unit and made an appreciable difference to the top speed.

At 1582cc (96.50cu in), the size remained the same, but the 9.0:1 compression ratio was higher than on the 60bhp (7.5:1) or 75bhp (8.5:1) engines, helping maximum power to be achieved higher up the scale, at 5500rpm. Two Zenith 32 NDIX carburettors were fitted to the Normal and Super versions of the 1600, but the Super 90 engine had two twin-choke Solex PII-4 carburettors. The Super 90 had the diameter of its inlet valves increased from 38mm (1.48in) to 40mm (1.56in) and the cylinder heads

Nipple-type hubcaps with the Porsche crest at their centres were fitted as standard to Supers from 1957 and were optional on Normal models. Radial tyres were standard from 1959.

The 1600 90bhp engine differed from the 1600 60bhp and 75bhp power units in having light alloy cylinder barrels and twin Solex 40 PII-4 carburettors instead of the standard Zenith 32 NDIX items.

were reworked to improve the flow of the fuel/air mixture to the cylinder bores.

To keep engine noise at an acceptable level, the less powerful cars still had cast iron cylinder barrels as standard, but the Super 90 had light alloy cylinders with a ferral surface to the bores. As usual, the pistons were made of alloy. Supplied either by Mahle or Kolbenschmidt, they were flat-topped with chamfered sides and had cut-outs for the valves. The main bearings on the regular 356B are as follows: numbers 1, 3 and 4 were light alloy bushes while number 2 was a split light alloy shell, but the Super 90 differed in having split steel-backed lead-coated shells for numbers 1, 2 and 3 and a light alloy bush for number 4. The piston rings were modified, and where the 356A had made do with two compression rings and one oil scraping ring, the 356B had an additional compression ring. To distinguish the Super 90 from the two other pushrod units it had a silver painted fan housing, rather than black. The cooling fan was made more efficient on the T6 model: the T5 (and 356A) engines had drawn in air at the rate of 560

litres per second at 4000rpm, but the rate was now 620 litres per second at 4000rpm.

With the 110mph Super 90, Porsche was able to keep the 356 competitive with other cars. Many people at the time, journalists and customers alike, regarded the Super 90 as the best car Porsche had ever produced, and many still do. The additional power was welcomed, but typically the modifications to the 1600 engine were not at the expense of reliability. The alloy cylinder barrels made the engine noisier, but a little racket is acceptable when it comes from a classic air-cooled flat-four.

The 356 engine was reaching the end of its development life by the end of 1962. With the Super 90 pushrod engine, Porsche had achieved as much as it could in performance without sacrificing reliability and longevity. The engine was tractable, developed reasonable torque (except below 3000rpm), offered excellent acceleration and a top speed which was more than sufficient. The 60bhp and 75bhp engines were also perfectly adequate for devotees of the marque, and, whichever version one chose, enthusiastic drivers sufficiently skilled could not only have fun, but take on cars with double the engine capacity and horsepower and beat them.

TRANSMISSION

Porsche experienced problems with the gearbox when it introduced the 356B. To begin with, the nose of the gearbox was damped by a single rubber mounting to simplify production and make life easier for mechanics, but this led to unsatisfactory levels of vibration and noise in the cabin. From the beginning of 1960, the single mounting was replaced by two, as in the earlier T2 model.

The gearbox was given the code number 741 and had the usual four forward speeds and reverse. Some rival manufacturers, including Alfa Romeo, were producing five-speed 'boxes by this time, but despite the absence of a fifth gear, many of Europe's top motoring writers regarded the Porsche 'blocking' synchromesh system as the best gearbox in the world. It was almost impossible to beat the synchromesh, no matter how hard or fast one moved the gearstick through the gate.

The 180mm (7.02in) diaphragm clutch remained the same on the 1600 Normal and Super, but the Super 90 was treated to a new 200mm (7.80in) Haeussermann diaphragm clutch. Intended to cope with the extra engine power, this coincided with a number of interesting chassis changes.

The ratios for gearboxes 644 and 716 were as follows: first 3.09:1, second 1.76:1, third 1.13:1, fourth 0.81:1, reverse 3.56:1 and final drive 4.428:1. The early 356B gearbox (type 741) with a single front mounting and the later twin front mounting type both had the same ratios as the earlier 356A gearbox, except that the third ratio in the 1600S and the Super 90 was slightly taller.

SUSPENSION

The main change, but standard only on the Super 90, was the addition of a compensating spring at the rear. This wonderfully simple but highly effective device keeps the rear wheels flatter on the road by assisting the torsion bars when under load. The compensating spring became an optional extra on other models and was even made available as a kit.

A curved piece of steel that runs transversely across the car and directly under the middle of the gearbox, the compensating spring is secured by a central support bracket with studs to the side covers of the gearbox. Further brackets and studs secure each of the outer ends of the spring to the two main radius arms on each side of the car. When this modification was introduced the rear torsion bars were 'softened up' by being reduced in diameter from 24mm to 23mm. This was to try to enhance some of

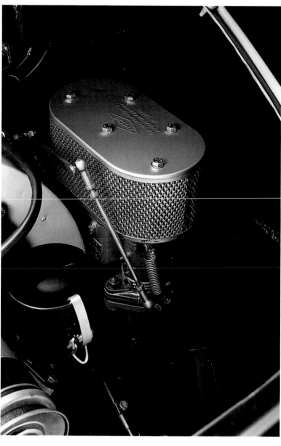

Impressively large mesh-type air filters protect the twin Solex 40 PII-4 carburettors of the '90' model.

the ride comfort taken away by the compensating spring which had the effect of stiffening the rear end. The softer 23mm torsion bars also came as part of the compensating spring fitting kit available for the 'lesser' models.

In practice the spring reduced the tendency of the swing-axles to jack themselves up under hard cornering and cause a wheel to adopt the dangerous 'tuck-in' position. The design of the rear suspension was thought responsible and Porsche even considered redesigning the whole system for a more conventional one, but the compensating spring acted as an inexpensive solution.

For anyone wishing to update a car with one of these kits, and original ones are not easy to find, great care must be exercised in removing the original torsion bars. As they are rising rate springs held under compression in their protective tubes, they are capable of inflicting severe injuries upon inexperienced operators. If in doubt it is best to seek the services of a Porsche expert.

The Super 90 was also fitted with Dutch-made Koni adjustable shock absorbers which, in conjunction with radial tyres, really transformed the car's roadholding and driveability. The easiest way to adjust these shock absorbers is to remove them from the car and place them in a vice, where they can be stiffened by pressing the top downwards and turning it anti-clockwise until the adjusting lug inside the body of the shock absorbers fits into the valve. The stiffness can be reduced by screwing the top half in an opposite clockwise direction.

Although there was nothing much wrong with the roadholding capabilities of the 356 before, the chassis modifications made to the Super 90 were absolutely stunning. The car was capable of going round corners at abnormally high speeds, as if on rails, and the more knowledgeable motoring journalists raved about it.

STEERING

The steering box, steering damper, tie-rods and the rest of the steering mechanism all remained unaltered. However, as road safety had become more of a public issue by the end of the 1950s, the steering wheel became dished, with the spokes angled away from the driver towards the steering boss, with the idea of decreasing the likelihood of serious chest injuries in an accident as well as improving the steering wheel aesthetically. The stalk for the headlamp flasher and indicators was now integrated into the steering column itself.

BRAKES

Despite the increasing popularity of disc brakes with many other sports car manufacturers, Porsche continued to fit drums to the 356B. There was a small modification, the outer casing of the drums now having 72 axial fins to assist heat dissipation. In virtually all rear-engined cars, apart from the later 911 Porsches with their ABS brakes, the rear weight bias encourages the front wheels to lock up under heavy braking. By improved cooling to the drums, Porsche went some way to alleviating the problem of brake fade, but never fully cured the tendency of the front brakes to lock up. The diameter of the drums was still 280mm (10.92in) and the width of the shoes remained 40mm (1.56in).

CONCLUSION

Porsche produced 30,963 examples of the 356B over four years, a considerable number for a small independent company, nearly 50 per cent more than the 21,045 examples of the 356A it had built between 1955 and 1959, and four times greater than the 7,627 original 356s made between 1950 and 1955. Despite this impressive increase the continuing search for improvement would lead to the final development of the air-cooled flat-four, the 356C, which had a relatively brief production run of two years before the introduction of the six-cylinder 911.

If the original 356 had set the scene for Porsche's future, and the 356A was perceived as the much improved 'Mark 2', the 356B was the mature, slightly flabbier, middle-aged version of Zuffenhausen's unique and slightly eccentric design. In essence the car remained true to Ferry Porsche's philosophy of 'leaving well alone if it works'. Escalating sales figures proved that Porsche was still on the right path with the 356B, which is why the basic shape of the bodywork and the chassis and engine configuration remained the same.

The 356 continued to be the driving choice for those enthusiasts who were looking for a challenge, something different from a 'run-of-the-mill' sports car. Its reputation for reliability and longevity had now become legendary and if things did go wrong, there was a superb dealer network to put things right. And, in keeping with a trend developed among Beetle owners, Porsche drivers were such a friendly, tightly-knit bunch that they waved and flashed their headlamps at each other on the road. In just a few years, the company had established itself as a manufacturer of truly great sports cars.

The 356B was the most successful Porsche yet, with 30,963 cars sold in four years.

THE 356C (1963-65)

While work on the forthcoming 901, later known as the 911, progressed, the 356C, announced in July 1963, provided 356 enthusiasts with an opportunity for a 'final fling' with an improved version of the car that had brought Porsche both an internationally respected name and a healthy bank account. The company had grown to be so successful that it was able to take over the Reutter coachbuilding concern on 1 March 1964. As a result, Reutter became Recaro and concentrated on the manufacture of car seats.

Changes to the new car were relatively few by Porsche's standards, because development had really gone as far as it could. There was no need to change the bodywork because Porsche knew that it was already aerodynamically efficient. Its rounded curves and wind-cheating appearance were an asset to the Porsche in an age when many other manufacturers were beginning to sharpen up their designs, an age in which sharp corners and flat surfaces became fashionable and where a chrome-encrusted radiator shell adorned with the maker's badge was often the only way of distinguishing one model from the next.

To many people in the motoring world, however, the 356 remained something of an enigma. The engine was still in the 'wrong' position and made an extraordinary noise, the dashboard was without a clutter of superfluous gauges or the polished plank of wood so beloved of the British, and practical rubber mats were still employed on the floor – no Wilton carpet here. Enthusiastic Porsche owners even had the audacity to enter sporting events and beat cars with double the engine capacity and power in what was, after all, a 'souped-up' Volkswagen Beetle.

The final version of the 356 body came with the introduction of the T6 in 1961 and all the modifications – twin air intakes on the enlarged rear lid, enlarged windscreen and rear window, bigger front lid and fresh-air louvres in the front scuttle – were carried through on the 356C. Wheels and hubcaps were modified to accommodate the newly-introduced disc brakes. Enlarging the rear window to improve rearward vision was an important step forward in the early 1960s and Porsche's engineers no doubt had good reasons for introducing a second air intake – but it is arguable whether either change improved the car aesthetically.

The cabriolet's appeal remained as strong as ever, sales accounting for around a fifth of total 356C production. Despite the inevitability of putting on weight, the cabriolet's superb lines ensured that it always looked impressive whether the top was up or down. This car is owned by Bill Stephens.

Cars fitted with the 75bhp engine were badged 'C' and those with the 95bhp engine were badged 'SC'.

Fresh air ventilation for the cabin was provided through louvres in the scuttle (right), a modification introduced on the T6. Wiper arms were originally painted silver, not black. Opening rear side windows (far right), first introduced in April 1951, were used until the end of production.

The front lid handle, with its evocative Porsche crest, remained unchanged from the 356B.

By the time the 356C had arrived, there were virtually no Volkswagen components left in the car's make-up, although for some the 356C was still the ultimate Beetle.

BODYSHELL & BODY TRIM

The body designed for the facelifted T6 model introduced in 1961 was carried through to the 356C. There were no changes to the external panels on the 356C, and apart from the scripts or badges on the rear panel which identified the revised cars as a 'Porsche C' or 'Porsche SC', it is actually impossible to distinguish between the later 356Bs and the 356C externally. After Porsche took over Reutter in March 1964, the 356C was no longer fitted with a coachbuilder's badge on the wing.

The steel chassis frame of the 356C was basically unaltered, but small changes took place in the rear bulkhead, which had a bracket mounting the cables for the new braking system, and in the shape of steel trays or pans underneath the modified rear seats.

The rear reflector could be fitted above the tail light or below the bumper according to customer preference.

In his autobiography, *Cars Are My Life*, Ferry Porsche wrote: 'It had been clear to me for a long time that we could not go on with the 356 for ever. We had to replace it; we had after all designed the car on the basis of VW components and made certain modifications to it in the course of the years. For example, we had added a new cylinder head with valves arranged in a V, aluminium cylinders with chrome-plated working surfaces, two carburettors on each side and a lot more besides. However, all these things were basically a temporary solution to the problem of getting better performance from the VW engine.'

The fuel tank was modified on left-hand drive cars on the introduction of the T6 with the filler neck being extended into the right-hand wing. Note that the spare wheel is correctly fastened with a leather strap. A typically thoughtful touch, a protective piece of vinyl was positioned inside the filler flap to protect the paintwork from being scratched by pump attendants.

The zip-out rear section of the cabriolet's hood was a T6 modification that was carried through to the 356C. To accommodate the factory-supplied hard-top, a modification was made to the rear compartment in 1958 and necessitated a change to the hood frame. Other than this, and the rear zipper fitted in 1961, the hood remained unchanged.

These restored seats, upholstery and hood bag are typical of the period in which the 356C was made. The tops of the seats shown here would originally have been made with a single piece of leather. Note that the seat belt is jointed in the rear compartment. All T6-bodied coupés and cabriolets have the added practicality of separate folding backrests for the rear seats.

For cars that were not specified with leather upholstery, a new type of softer leatherette was used for the seats.

Because of design problems owners of right-hand drive cars still had to open the front lid to gain access to the fuel tank (right). This special suitcase is a highly desirable period accessory. Rear air vents had been introduced on the 356B coupé to improve window demisting, but the openings were modified on the 356C (far right) to give a better spread of air over the glass.

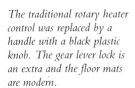

The traditional rotary heater control was replaced by a handle with a black plastic knob. The gear lever lock is an extra and the floor mats are modern.

INTERIOR TRIM

As beautifully stark and functional as ever, the interior, like the bodywork, changed very little. There were a number of rather trivial detail modifications carried out to the 356C, and in the case of the magnet added to the glovebox lid in addition to the normal lock, they were a trifle bizarre. This change is a typical example of how weight can be unnecessarily added to a motor car.

The front seat cushions were modified in shape to offer both the driver and passenger greater comfort and lateral thigh support, and the backrests of the rear seats were reduced in height. A plastic 'direc-

Armrests were fitted to both interior door panels (far left) as standard and the door cappings continued to be upholstered to match the rest of the interior trim. The small quarterlight handle (left) was fitted with a release button for greater security.

Obscuring the driver's view of the instruments, in this case with a full circular horn ring, was always a Porsche speciality on various 356 models.

Dashboard changes for the 356C included a magnetic catch for the glovebox lid, minor changes to the switchgear and a red handbrake warning light incorporated into the combination gauge – the functional cockpit remained unmistakably Porsche.

The standard 356C wheels had flat hubcaps and were mildly modified in shape to suit the use of disc brakes.

now required just one flick of the hand. The new heater control lever was fitted with a small black knob on its leading edge.

WHEELS & TYRES

Because of the change from drum to all-round disc brakes, the road wheels had to be modified in shape to fit the hubs, although to a casual observer they probably looked much the same. The five-stud fixings, and the simple style of the wheels with ten roughly oval vents to aid cooling to the brakes, were retained. It is interesting that Porsche stuck to its distinctively plain and functional steel wheels right down to the last 356, especially in view of the fact that by this time many other manufacturers had adopted rather prettier alloy wheels for their more sporting cars.

It might appear that the factory was being typically cautious about new-fangled items like alloy wheels, but it is now clear that Porsche were developing alloys for the new 911 well before the demise of the 356. It is also probable that the now familiar Fuchs five-spoke alloys that have characterised the 911 series for more than 30 years were fitted for experimental purposes to some 356s during the latter days of the car's production.

In *Porsche Past & Present*, Denis Jenkinson wrote as follows about Porsche's role in the Targa Florio: 'While the actual racing cars in the workshops were of prime importance, there were always other things to see such as experimental brakes, wheels, exhaust systems, body panels, carburettor changes, gearbox alterations and so on. If you saw what appeared to be a normal 1600 SC or Super 90 coupé being used by one of the factory drivers for familiarisation with the Targa Florio circuit, and if, when he got back to Cefalu, it was then wheeled into the workshop or taken round the back of the hotel, it was worth following to see what was going on. Disc brakes, five-speed gearboxes, new rear suspensions, alloy wheels and so on could all be inspected before they went into production.'

This illustrates how firmly Porsche believed that the best way to discover the true value of new components, and especially ones like alloy wheels, was to test them thoroughly, preferably in motor sport, before they were let loose on the car-buying public. The rationale behind this was clear: if new alloy wheels could withstand the hammering of a mountain circuit like the Targa Florio, they would certainly be safe enough in normal road use. But sadly this was one of several developments that came too late for the 356C. It soldiered on with plain steel wheels, painted silver in standard trim or chrome-plated on the Carrera version. The width of the road wheels remained the same at 4½in and the diameter was unaltered at 15in, although the hubcaps became

tion' scoop over the vents in each side of the rear window fed warm air to the glass more efficiently. Armrests were provided on both doors as standard equipment and the plastic-covered passenger grab handle next to the glovebox was more angled, to make it easier to grip. As with the 356B, carpeting was generously provided seemingly everywhere except on the floor, and was coloured dark grey.

INSTRUMENTS & CONTROLS

There were a number of small changes to the switchgear. The light switch, which had been between the tachometer and the speedometer, was repositioned to the right of the speedometer. The tachometer, previously a conventional mechanical device, became electrically operated from May 1964. The cigar lighter, previously to the right of the radio, was moved immediately to the right of the ashtray on the extension to the dashboard below the radio. There was also a change in the shape of the courtesy light from an oval to a rectangle, and instead of being operated by a conventional switch, it was now turned on and off by rocking the whole unit from side to side.

One function that distinguishes the 356C from all previous models is the heater control lever. The floor-mounted rotating knob that had served for so long was changed for a lever placed directly in front of the gear lever, and admitting heat to the cabin

slightly flatter as a result of the change in shape, and radial tyres were, of course, fitted as standard.

ELECTRICS

From May 1964 the 356C was fitted with an electric tachometer in place of the more traditional mechanical one, a production change that also coincided with a switch from 6-volt to 12-volt electrics. To run the new system, a larger Bosch battery was installed in the luggage compartment and the various electrical components throughout the car were uprated. All the electrical equipment was made and supplied by Bosch as usual. The starter motor was an EED 0.5/6 L35, the dynamo was an LJ/GEG200/12/2700L5 and the regulator was an RS/ua200/12/23. Standard headlamp bulbs were rated the same as the 6-volt system at a dismal 45/40 watts.

ENGINE

As Porsche began to leave its Volkswagen origins behind, the lower-powered 1600 60bhp Normal engine was dropped from the range and the regular pushrod-engined cars were limited to just two models: the 75bhp 'C' and the 95bhp 'SC', both engines being developments of those they replaced. The cylinder heads were reworked with new inlet and exhaust port shapes for enhanced flow of the fuel/air mixture, and the SC version was fitted with sodium-filled valves to help heat dissipation at the cylinder heads, an important consideration for an air-cooled engine with this kind of power.

Describing an engine with 95bhp as powerful may seem exaggerated, considering that the average family saloon in the 1990s develops about the same, but this was more than 30 years ago.

The 1600C engine developed its maximum 75bhp at 5200rpm, had a compression ratio of 8.5:1 and received fuel via twin Zenith 32 NDIX twin-choke carburettors. The SC version had a higher compression ratio of 9.5:1, produced its 95bhp at 5800rpm and was fitted with two Solex PJJ-4 twin-choke carburettors. An important difference between the two engines was the cylinder barrel construction: the C had conventional cast iron cylinders, while the SC was fitted with light alloy barrels with iron liners.

On the C engine the diameter of the inlet valves remained at 38mm (1.48in) while the diameter of the exhaust valves was increased from 31mm (1.21in) to 34mm (1.33in). On the SC, the diameter of the inlet valve increased to 40mm (1.56in) and that of the exhaust valve was also 34mm (1.33in). Such modifications to the engines helped to make these cars even better to drive than their predecessors.

A modified camshaft profile on the 75bhp engine made the car more tractable at low speeds and offered a better spread of usable power across nearly all the rev range. This was also true with the 95bhp car, which was renowned for being particularly smooth, especially in the upper rev ranges, because it was also fitted with a counter-weighted crankshaft that coped admirably with the vibrations inherent in a four-cylinder power unit.

The benefits of the new engines could best be appreciated when accelerating between 60mph and 90mph in top gear, both possessing the ability to pull smoothly and quickly especially when overtaking slower traffic. Porsche claimed a top speed for the C version of around 109mph with the car reaching 60mph in 14sec, and this was subsequently confirmed in road tests by several motoring publications. Not surprisingly, the SC model was rather faster, with a top speed in the region of 116mph and reaching 60mph in around 13sec.

Despite the increases in power for the revised pushrod engines, fuel consumption remained as impressive as ever. At cruising speeds, 31mpg was easily obtainable, although in everyday driving conditions this would fall to about 25mpg. Exactly the same figures applied to contemporary 1200 Volkswagen Beetles, the Porsche's superior aerodynamic shape clearly compensating for its more powerful engine.

TRANSMISSION

Both the C and SC models were fitted with the 200mm (7.8in) diaphragm clutch already used on the Super 90. The new clutch differed from the old 180mm (7.0in) unit in that the thickness of the driven plate was increased from 9.1mm (0.35in) to 9.5mm (0.37in), the clutch recess in the flywheel was increased to 205mm (8.0in) and in depth to 25mm (0.97in), and the diameter of the springs was increased from 150mm (5.85in) to 165mm (6.44in). The gearbox now had to cope with more power from the engine and the idea behind these clutch improvements was to improve the reliability of the transmission. The gearbox retained the twin mountings at the front and, in all other respects, remained unaltered from the 356B T6.

SUSPENSION

The ingenious rear compensating spring which had been designed with such success for the Super 90 was dropped on the 356C, although it remained available on special order.

Porsche began to feel that its customers, particularly in the American market, required an altogether softer suspension system and greater ride comfort, and so revised torsion bars were fitted. At the rear, each bar was reduced in length from 627mm (24.45in) to 522mm (20.36in) and in diameter from

As the 60bhp engine had
been dropped, the only
pushrod engines available
were the 75bhp unit (above)
and the 95bhp engine, which
was a development of the
Super 90.

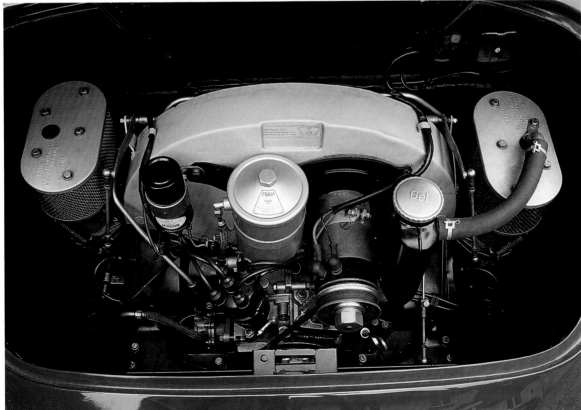

When modified to give
95bhp, the 1600 engine was
reliable, tractable and
provided enthusiastic drivers
with brisk performance, but it
represented the tuning limit
for an air-cooled four-cylinder
pushrod engine in the early
1960s.

24mm (0.94in) – or 23mm (0.90in) if a compensating spring was fitted – to 20mm (0.86in). A large rubber bump stop was also fitted above the driveshafts on each side of the car to keep axle travel in check and the inner wings were slightly reshaped accordingly. To compensate for sogginess introduced at the rear, the front anti-roll bar was stiffened by being increased in diameter by 1mm (0.04in).

STEERING

Yet again, the layout of the well proven steering gear remained unaltered, except that a Guibo coupling was fitted between the steering gearbox bolted to the torsion bar tube and the steering column itself. The Guibo coupling, which was made of thick rubber, assisted the steering damper in minimising the effect of vibrations from the road wheels through to the steering wheel, and replaced the old, much thinner Volkswagen-style rubber disc.

BRAKES

At last, drums were changed for discs on all four wheels, although it is believed that the first 200 or so 356Cs were actually fitted with drums.

Good as the drum brakes undoubtedly were, disc brakes made a significant difference to the stopping power of the 356C. Made under licence by ATE to a conventional Dunlop design, the discs are 227mm (8.85in) in diameter at the front and 243mm (9.48in) at the rear, with a 180mm (7.02in) drum cast into the centre of rear brakes for the cable-operated handbrake.

The separate fluid reservoir for the new braking system was positioned inside the luggage compartment to the right of the spare wheel instead of being positioned on top of the master cylinder as previously. The master cylinder was fitted with a spring-loaded conical valve with a small hole at its centre, in order to allow the hydraulics to become de-pressurised when the brake pedal was released. The master cylinders on the previous drum-braked cars are different from those on the 356Cs, which can be distinguished by an identification plate that reads 'Zylinder hat Spezial-Bodenventil' ('This cylinder has a purging check valve').

Entirely conventional, the calipers were made in two halves, each side comprising a dust cover with a clamping ring, a piston with a sealing ring and the cylinder. The brake pads, secured by retaining pins, a cross spring and clips, were 15mm (0.59in) in thickness, and new ones were recommended when they had wore down to no more than 2mm (0.08in).

As one would expect, the disc brakes fitted to the 356C were made to the highest standards and performed well under normal driving conditions, although excessive use by a spirited driver over sev-

eral thousands of miles could cause discs to crack or warp. For restorers today, new brake discs should be between 10.3mm (0.40in) and 10.5mm (0.41in) in thickness at the front and between 9.8mm (0.38in) and 10mm (0.39in) at the rear. Superficial damage to the surface of the discs can be machined providing the width of the disc is not reduced by more than 5mm (0.19in), but it should not be assumed that the grooving that appears to affect all discs over time is the result of damage.

The arrival of all-round disc brakes improved the 356C's stopping power out of recognition. The rear discs (lower picture) were cast with a drum for the handbrake in their centres. First introduced as standard equipment on the Super 90, Koni shock absorbers transformed the handling.

CONCLUSION

After a production run of 16,668, the 356C was finally discontinued in 1965 to make way for the new six-cylinder 911 and its closely related 912 four-cylinder sister. Karmann at Osnabrück ceased 356 production on 21 January and the Porsche-owned Reutter factory finished on 28 April. The Zuffen-hausen works also said farewell to the 356 on 28 April with the production of the final cabriolet.

In 15 years, the 356 had established the name of Porsche all over the world. Writing in *Sports Car World* in 1965, Bill Tuckey stated: 'The Porsche has the best gearbox, the best finish, one of the most efficient bodies and the lowest wear index of any sports car in the world, regardless of price. Not as fast as some, not as spectacular as others, it does its job better and more efficiently than any other sports car in the world.'

Time and again, the 356 was praised for the quality of its finish, panel fit, engineering integrity and, towards the end of its life, its remarkable roadholding capabilities. Its shape had a unique appeal, typically functional styling quite unlike the seductive Italian mode. An individualist's machine, it was given to the world by a family of genius.

The 356C was the ultimate development of the theme, but in some ways it became a victim of its own success. As Porsche ownership increased and broadened, the very reasons why it sold so well in the first place could now be perceived disadvantages. As a small two-seater it now appealed to a growing minority – although potential customers were still looking for individual looks and good performance they also wanted a car that could carry a decent quantity of luggage.

Not only that, the performance of the 356 was beginning to look a little less startling by the mid-1960s, when the rest of the world's manufacturers were extracting similar power from sporting saloons. The Lotus Cortina was one and, fitted with a 1600 twin-cam twin-carburettor engine developing 105bhp, was capable of 108mph. This was not quite as fast as the 356 and certainly could not match its quality of engineering, but it cost considerably less to buy, had four seats and a large boot for luggage.

The only course open to the talented engineers in Stuttgart was to produce a completely new car. The 911, officially announced in 1964 as a direct successor to the 356, had more power, more room in the rear and a boot capable of swallowing a full set of golf clubs. Thirty years on, the 911 is still in production but perhaps it too, like its illustrious forebear, will soon have outlived its usefulness.

The end of the line. A cabriolet was available throughout the life of the 356, but it took nearly 20 years, curiously, for the 911 that came next to be offered with this body style.

THE FOUR-CAM CARRERA (1955-65)

*P*orsche's racing and rallying history is quite another story, but no book about the 356 would be complete without reference to the famous four-cam engine designed by Ernst Fuhrmann. By the early 1950s Porsches had already risen to great heights in various sporting competitions with 'works' and private entries, but good as the pushrod engines undoubtedly were, their development potential was severely limited. For serious competition work at top level, something more powerful was needed if Porsche was going to stand a chance. The obvious route to more power was to enlarge the existing engine, but Fuhrmann was aware of the limited ability of a pushrod unit to produce high revs and therefore set about designing an engine which would dispense with pushrods.

Design number 547, this engine was a flat-four air-cooled unit like its Volkswagen-derived sisters, but the cylinder heads were to a completely new and ingenious design. Each pair of cylinders has two gear-driven overhead camshafts which operate the

valves via finger followers. The valves themselves are set in a 78 degree V-shape. The lower of the two camshafts in each cylinder head operates the exhaust valves and the upper one operates the inlets. As befits a competition engine, the two halves of the crankcase, the cylinder barrels and cylinder heads were all made of light alloy. In keeping with traditional Porsche practice, the running surfaces of the bores were chrome-plated to reduce friction and a Hirth roller-bearing crankshaft was chosen in place of a plain-bearing unit.

In its original 1498cc (91.38cu in) form, the new engine had an 85mm (3.32in) bore and a 66mm (2.57in) stroke, produced a maximum 100bhp at 6200rpm, and was developed in secrecy. Porsche even kept quiet about its 'secret weapon' when it went to the Nürburgring in 1953 with the new unit installed in an open-top 550 Spyder racing car, waiting instead until the Paris Motor Show later in the year to announce it officially to the public. It caused a sensation. There was nothing particularly new

Primarily intended for racing, the Carrera 356 was launched in 1955 and fitted with the Fuhrmann-designed 1500 four-cam engine that had previously seen service in the 550 Spyder racing cars. This English-registered car owned by Fred Hampton is one of the earliest Carreras made.

The GT version of the Carrera, with light alloy doors and lids, became available in 1957 and looked sensational, whether standing still or being driven in anger. Around 100 GTs are thought to have been built between 1957-64. Interesting GT details are the lack of a Carrera script on the front wings and different wheels with steel centres rivetted to aluminium rims.

Despite the Carrera script, it is obvious from the additional louvres in the engine lid (right) that this is no ordinary 356. A 'belt and braces' job, leather straps (far right) on some GTs gave extra security against the front lid popping open, and were required under international racing regulations. Again to save weight, it was usual for Carrera owners to remove the bumpers.

To save weight, the side and rear windows on the GT version were made of Plexiglass, and the opening rear quarter windows had no frames (right). Note that GTs had quarterlights in the front side windows. In the absence of a wind-up mechanism, a leather strap is used to move the Plexiglass side windows (far right).

A larger 80-litre fuel tank, known as the GT tank, was an extra-cost option from 1956, but when fitted to the Carrera its extra weight, especially when full, partially negated the advantage of the GT's alloy body panels. Because this car has been fitted with dual-circuit brakes for extra safety, it has two master cylinders instead of one as originally. Because this Carrera GT was a works test vehicle, its lightweight front lid hinges (right) are believed to be unique.

An ex-works car raced by Huschke von Hanstein, this 1959-spec 356A Carrera is fitted with a plain-bearing four-cam engine and is owned by English enthusiast and collector Mike Smith.

about overhead camshafts, but here was an engine with no fewer than four of them. In addition there was a dual-ignition system with two sparking plugs per cylinder, two coils, two distributors (driven directly by the inlet camshafts) and two twin-choke Solex PJJ carburettors.

It was with this engine in a 550 Spyder that Hans Hermann and Herbert Linge finished sixth overall in the 1954 Mille Miglia and won the 1500cc sports car category. Further success came in the same year when Hermann won his class and finished a magnificent third overall in the Carrera Panamericana, a gruelling high-speed road race through Mexico which Porsche considered so important that it referred thereafter to the four-cam engine as the 'Carrera' – Spanish for 'race'.

Of course the 550 Spyder racing car was not a sensible proposition for most of Porsche's customers, and so now the aim was to make the engine available in a 356 bodyshell. First, it had to be tested properly

Similar in shape to Speedster seats, the simple GT seats were in aluminium on hardwood frames and gave excellent lateral support. Originally the seat centres would have been trimmed in black or grey corduroy. The fire extinguisher is a sensible precaution against a valuable piece of Stuttgart history disappearing in a cloud of smoke.

The Carrera's dashboard layout was essentially the same as the less exotic Porsches, but the speedometer and tachometer calibrations were higher. This works test car has an additional oil pressure gauge in the centre, a separate fuel pump switch, and a VDM steering wheel of a design and rim colour used only on works cars. A double indicator and headlamp flasher switch is also fitted on the column.

With its Weber DCM3 carburettors and plain-bearing crankshaft, the 1600 four-cam engine (above) is a much easier animal to tame than the original 1500 unit. The huge air boxes under the rear lid were made from hand-beaten aluminium and mated to shrouds round the carburettor air trumpets, missing on this GT Carrera but visible on the red one (right).

and for this Porsche chose the challenging Liège-Rome-Liège Rally of 1954. One of the old alloy-bodied Gmünd coupes was fitted with the new 'four-cammer' and entrusted to Herbert Linge and Helmut Polensky. If the engine could survive this event, which included long and arduous sections in the Alps, it could survive anything and could be pronounced fit for Porsche's most demanding customers. Polensky and Linge brought the car home in first place and Porsche decided to press ahead with a production version.

The 356A/1500GS four-cam was the result and made its public debut at the 1955 Frankfurt Motor Show. It was known as the Carrera, like subsequent 'hot' versions of production Porsches until the com-

pany's marketing department decided to devalue the name by applying it to ordinary models. Before the demise of the 356 in 1965, the four-cam engine was developed considerably, being increased in size first to 1.6 litres and eventually to a full 2-litre unit.

Carreras differ from the regular 356s in having dry sump lubrication and front-mounted electric fuel pumps. The oil tank is positioned under the left-hand rear wing and oil from the crankcase is delivered to it by a scavenge pump. For winter use, it was necessary to fit a piece of foam rubber between the oil tank and its attendant stone guard to prevent the oil from becoming over-cooled in the air stream. One small difference between the engines of the racing cars and those of the coupés was that the compression ratio was reduced from 9.5:1 to 9.0:1.

The four-cam engine was initially available in the coupé and Speedster bodies, with lightweight GT versions offered in 1955 for the Speedster and from 1957 for the coupé. In contrast to the de luxe model, the GT was intended for serious competition work and had lighter Speedster seats and Perspex windows (apart from the windscreen). There were no window winders (the door windows were held in place with leather straps similar to those on the Speedster), no rear seats and no heater. All Carreras had different instruments, with the speedometer calibrated to 160mph for Britain and North America or 250kph for Europe, and the tachometer red-lined at 6000rpm but reading to 8000rpm.

Aluminium was used for the doors (lined on the

The Carrera's front brake drums (far left) were 'borrowed' from the 550 Spyder and were 20mm wider than the 40mm drums fitted to the standard cars. Because the rear drums (left) were narrower than those at the front, they were fitted with a 20mm spacer to balance up the track.

inside with cardboard) and front and rear lids, the latter bearing a gold-coloured 'Carrera' badge. GT versions were distinguished by having two banks of louvres (five slots on the 1500, six on the 1600) either side of the normal central intake, and large ducts on the underside of the rear lid to take air to the carburettors.

The racing Spyder's more powerful brakes, which had 60mm (2.36in) front shoes in place of the standard 40mm (1.57in) items, were also fitted, and both the GT and de luxe ran on larger 5.90 × 15in tyres instead of the 5.60 × 15in tyres used on the standard 356s. Both versions had twin Solex 40PJJ-4 carbu-

rettors and ran with a compression ratio of 9.0:1, but power outputs differed. Whereas the de luxe road version produced 100bhp at 6200rpm, the GT developed 110bhp at 6400rpm – the difference can be attributed to camshaft and ignition tuning.

Like all highly-tuned race-bred cars, the Carrera demanded to be driven, and driven hard. It was a car that needed to be picked up by the scruff of the neck and booted. It needed to be revved: a clear case of having to be cruel to be kind. However, many of Porsche's customers had not appreciated the true nature of their Carreras and those who were content to potter about at low revs soon paid a heavy penalty.

A classic among classics. The 'boxer' configuration of the all-alloy Carrera motor can be clearly seen. Early engines, like this one, were fitted with Solex PJJ-4 carburettors.

Two plugs per cylinder are fed by two distributors – one on the rear of each inlet camshaft. Later cars have crankshaft-driven distributors. Note the cooling fins on the lower of the two camboxes.

Beautifully made and impenetrably complex, the camshafts are driven by shafts and bevel gears and each cam acts on finger-type followers. Maintenance and rebuilds must be left to acknowledged experts.

The roller-bearing crankshafts regularly failed and the plugs oiled up. But this was rarely the case with drivers who made the most of their cars. However, the Carrera got an early reputation for being unreliable and Porsche set about modifying the engine.

Displacing 1587.5cc (96.84cu in), the 1.6-litre version (Type 692) which appeared in mid-1958 retained the 66mm (2.57in) stroke of the 1.5-litre but the bore was increased to 87.5mm (3.41in), and a plain-bearing crankshaft took the place of the more

usual roller-bearing one. With the same Solex carburettors as the 1500 version and a compression ratio of 9.0:1, maximum power of 105bhp was produced at 6500rpm. Because the plain-bearing crankshaft was subjected to higher running temperatures, the Carrera was now fitted with two oil coolers mounted at the front of the car behind the horn grilles. The system was regulated by an oil thermostat or 'oilstat'. Other modifications to the revised engine included the drive for the distributors:

instead of being driven by the inlet camshafts, they were positioned in front of the cooling fan and driven by a shaft and helical gears from the crankshaft. This move not only reduced the vibrations inherent in the previous system but also allowed the engine to be timed more accurately.

Because the Carrera was so noisy inside the cabin, it proved to be considerably less popular than Porsche had envisaged. The de luxe version was more civilised as a road car than the GT, but even so it was still considered tiring to drive and was dropped when the 356B was introduced in 1959. By this time

it had a compression ratio of 9.8:1, two twin-choke Weber 40 DCM carburettors and developed 115bhp at 6500rpm. Some considered that Porsche had shot itself in the foot with the Carrera at this stage because the 356B Super 90 fitted with a conventional pushrod engine was almost as fast, considerably more tractable and easier to drive.

In skilled hands the 1500 or 1600 Carreras were extremely rewarding motor cars, but because they developed most of their power in the upper rev ranges they were not really suited to everyday road use. As usual, Porsche went some way to silencing its

The Carrera 2 fitted with the 2-litre four-cam engine, announced in 1961 and made available from early 1962, is for some the ultimate 356 road car.

Gold-coloured Carrera 2 tail script is one of very few external give-aways that something special lurks beneath the rear lid. 'Big-bore' tail pipes and air vents in the valance give a hint that this is not one of the regular cars. Note the position of the reversing light.

The adjustable head restraints are mounted on brackets fastened to the rear of the seats. Carrera 2s came with the folding rear seats that were originally introduced on the 356B in 1959.

The Carrera 2 was not as fast as the E-type Jaguar, which was also announced in 1961, but its sizzling performance and 130mph top speed capability was extracted from just 1966cc.

critics. In the spring of 1962, the Carrera 2 with its enlarged four-cam 2-litre engine was to become the ultimate road-going development of the 356. Although there were only 436 examples, all in the B and C series, it is one of the rarest and most desirable of all Porsches. With the same configuration as the 1600 four-cam unit, the 2-litre had a bore of 92mm (3.59in) and a stroke of 74mm (2.89in), producing an overall size of 1966cc (119.93cu in). A high compression ratio of 9.5:1 was used and a maximum 130bhp was produced at 6200rpm. Plain bearings continued to be used for the crankshaft.

The cylinder barrels were once again in light alloy but with a ferral coating on the bores. Outwardly, the unit can be distinguished by its exceptionally large, square, wire-mesh air filters and square cambox covers. There were two twin-choke Solex 40 PII-4 carburettors. Capable of well over 120mph and 0-60mph in less than 10sec, the Carrera 2 may have had 'hooligan' tendencies, but it was a real driver's car, at its best on a twisting, fast road. The 356B 2000GS and GT versions, which were intended for competition, produced 140bhp and 155bhp respectively. Both ran on twin Weber 46 JDM twin-choke

The sumptuous seats on this Carrera 2 are fitted with head restraints, which were listed as accessories from 1955. The Carrera's tachometer is red-lined at 7000rpm and calibrated to 8000rpm, while the speedometer reads to an optimistic 160mph. The beautiful steering wheel is a wood-rimmed Nardi.

carburettors and had a compression ratio of 9.8:1. The difference in power output between the two cars was, once again, down to engine tuning 'tweaks'. The GT version, for example, was fitted with a sports exhaust system whereas the GS used the standard exhaust.

ITALIAN DIVERSION

Towards the end of the 1950s it had become apparent to the Porsche management hierarchy, who remained as enthusiastic about international motor sport as ever, that their existing cars, even in Carrera form, were beginning to struggle against opposition from Italy and Britain. Porsche's engines remained competitive in the horsepower stakes, but the cars had generally put on weight in the interest of driver and passenger comfort. The solution, therefore, was to produce a lightweight racer, and the idea for the two-seater GTL version was born as a result of a meeting between Ferry Porsche and Carlo Abarth in September 1959. Fashioned over a wooden buck by the Italian body builders, Zagato of Turin, the all-

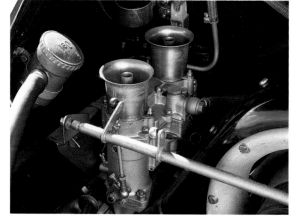

A mass of mind-boggling complexity, the 1966cc four-cam engine develops a maximum 130bhp at 6200rpm. Unlike the earlier Carreras, the distributors are driven from the crankshaft rather than the camshafts, and are situated at the rear of the engine. This regular version of the Carrera was fitted with Solex 40 PII-4 carburettors whereas the GT had 46 JDM Webers. Note the position of the oil filler.

new aluminium body was designed largely by Franco Scaglione (who previously had worked for Bertone) to fit an existing 356B chassis, the work being overseen by Abarth. The body was 5in (127mm) lower and 4.7in (119mm) narrower than a standard 356B, and overall the Abarth version was a staggering 100kg (220lb) lighter too. Porsche placed an initial order for 20 of these exotic lightweights,

The spartan interior of the Abarth Carrera had a different dashboard, but the binnacle ahead of the driver housed Porsche instruments.

which were intended as even quicker versions of the existing four-cam Carreras.

Initially, the car was something of a disaster. The prototype had been built in a hurry, in the manner of nearly all prototype racing cars of the day, and was clearly not up to Porsche's usual standards. The body leaked water and the driving position was typically Italian – built for people with long arms, short legs and tapered heads. If nothing else, though, the body was exceptionally pretty, aerodynamically efficient and smooth. Perspex covers could be fitted to fair in the standard 356 headlamps, and the engine lid was

fitted with a neat opening flap for occasions when the engine needed additional cooling. This flap was eventually supplemented with myriad louvres, which rather spoiled the smooth appearance of the coupé bodyshell but did the job efficiently.

The GTL, or Abarth Carrera as it became known, was fitted with the plain-bearing 1.6-litre engine and customers had a choice of three levels of tune – 115bhp, 128bhp or 135bhp. The range of power outputs was the result of different jet settings in the carburettors and a choice of three different exhaust systems – standard, sports or Sebring. Because it was some 20kg (44lb) lighter than Porsche's conventional Carrera, it was typically more than a second faster over 0-60mph and could reach a top speed in the region of 130mph (210kph). Naturally, the interior of the car was sparsely appointed (and utilised several existing Porsche components), but it was fitted with a headlining.

Despite Porsche's initial misgivings, the car proved to be successful. It scored a class win and sixth overall upon its debut in the 1960 Targa Florio in the hands of Herbert Linge and Paul Strähle, and took another class win at the Nürburgring a couple of weeks later. There was also a class win and tenth place overall in June at the Le Mans 24 Hours, where the car reached a top speed of 138mph (222kph) on the Mulsanne straight.

Just that initial batch of 20 lightweight GTs was built under the Abarth banner. The chassis numbers range from 1001 to 1021. Now highly collectable, the GTL was superseded in 1962 by the 718/2 coupé, which in turn gave way to the highly specialised glassfibre-bodied 904 racer in 1964.

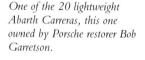

One of the 20 lightweight Abarth Carreras, this one owned by Porsche restorer Bob Garretson.

THE SPECIAL CONVERTIBLES (1954-62)

It was clear from the start that Porsche would produce a soft-top version of the coupé, as both the prototype and the first production models were open-top cars. The pretty two-seater design lent itself well to a cabriolet, the nicely proportioned lines of the body being well able to accept a roof transplant. Naturally, the cabriolet cost a little more than its 'tin-top' sister, but after the war the market for 'fresh-air' motoring grew steadily, particularly in the sunnier parts of Europe and America, and Porsche was keen to capitalise on it.

Modifications to the cabriolet ran roughly parallel with those of the coupé, with a few obvious differences between the body types. For many enthusiasts, the 356 cabriolet represented the ultimate in motoring enjoyment, and today the convertibles are still highly desirable, commanding higher prices than the coupés despite their rust problems. However, to the Porsche purist, the cabriolet was and remains something of an enigma.

Denis Jenkinson made the following comments in his book *Porsche 356*: 'The low wind resistance was always an impressive thing about the 356, the wind noise in the coupé being incredibly low, and it was this efficient shape that appealed to me. I could not bring myself to accept the drophead versions, known as the Cabriolet and Roadster, or the Speedster, which was an open-top version with a primitive hood and side screens; the Cabriolet model with its detachable hardtop seemed to oppose all the good principles of Professor Porsche. I always felt that people who bought anything other than the standard coupé bodywork were not serious Porsche motorists.'

The coupé's steel chassis frame was so strong that the cabriolet did not require additional strengthening to prevent it flexing. Torsional rigidity was maintained so well that there was very little scuttle shake, compared with most other dropheads.

The cabriolet's hood was strong, well-made and almost totally weatherproof, in stark contrast to many British sports car of the day, which had little more than a piece of canvas loosely stretched over a rudimentary folding frame. By comparison, the hoods made by Reutter for Porsches were bespoke works of art. Largely unchanged throughout the 356's life, they were similar in construction to those made by Karmann at Osnabrück for the Beetle cabriolet.

The complex folding frame was made from steel and aluminium with a traditional wooden bow at the front and rear. The outer material was made from a closely-woven cotton fabric and, with the headlining, created a sandwich with a horsehair filling. Cabriolets built by Reutter had a glass rear window secured in a wooden frame, whereas the Heuer-built cars were distinguished by a narrow alloy trim around the perimeter of the rear window. The hood was secured at the rear by a piece of wood tacked to

the bulkhead, and at the front with a manual latch on each side of the car.

The hood fitted so well that sitting in a cabriolet felt rather like being in a coupé. To improve the fit at the front of the hood, a narrow fabricated steel panel, fitted to the wooden bow, protruded from the leading edge of the fabric. After the 356A was introduced, this panel was covered by the hood, which also acquired a more curved front at this time. Another change was a larger rear window in March 1957, when the hood became fastened at the rear by small swivelling 'rivets'. A zip in the back of the hood fitted to the T6 Cabriolet in 1961 allowed the rear window to be removed, providing ventilation in the cabin even with the hood up.

Elegant and understated, the style and feel of the 356 is unique among cabriolets, best appreciated from behind the steering wheel on a fine day with the hood down. However, its susceptibility to corrosion can make restoring a neglected or rusty example very expensive.

Just 16 examples of the alloy-bodied America Roadster were built by Heuer during 1952, and were intended for competition. Its 'hump-backed' styling and minimal equipment provided inspiration for the Speedster, introduced in 1954.

The Roadster's two-piece windscreen differs in design from the cabriolet version and there are no side windows in the doors.

AMERICA ROADSTER

The first Roadsters are something of an oddity in Porsche folklore. Produced in small numbers – no more than 16 are thought to have been built – for the American market, they were constructed by Heuer for just a few months in 1952 until that company folded. It is a pity but Reutter neither had the space nor manpower to take over production. It is also significant that they were not able to weld up the aluminium bodies. A strange beast with styling that gave inspiration for the later Speedster, the Roadster (Type 540) had a distinctive 'hump-back' body in aluminium, with a long, sweeping tail and cutaways in the doors. A hood was provided but, like that of the Speedster that followed, it was a primitive affair with a sheet of cotton attached to a folding frame.

Intended primarily for competition, the car was comparatively spartan in its other fixtures and fittings. And because the 16 cars were all hand-built, there appear to have been differences between each one. For example, the wheel arches, large semi-circles on the earliest Roadsters, were modified twice, first becoming slightly less rounded and then more closely resembling the normal production style. Interestingly, the majority of Roadsters had two air intake grilles in the rear lid, a modification which did not find its way onto the regular produc-

tion models until the introduction of the 356B T6.

Competition-minded owners particularly liked the Roadster's talent for being able to shed weight quickly. The glass windscreen, secured by two wing nuts and one bolt, could be removed and substituted for a Perspex one, saving 20lb (9kg). Aluminium bucket seats and leather bonnet straps also saved weight. In true amateur tradition, the Roadster could be driven to a sporting event, stripped of its hubcaps, hood, jack, tools, boot lining and other superfluous trim, take part in a race, and be driven home on public roads afterwards. In all, as much as 115lb (51kg) could be saved by the removal of these bits and pieces.

Fitted with the 1488cc (90.77cu in) pushrod engine developing 75bhp at 5500rpm, the Roadster ran with a compression ratio of 8.2:1 and was fitted with twin Solex 40PBIC carburettors. In this guise, the Roadster's top speed was some 10mph higher than a standard 356, and although no official figures are available, it was also considerably faster away from the starting blocks. According to John Bentley, who tested a Roadster in 1953 for *Auto Age*, the car had a power-to-weight ratio of 18.8lb/bhp, 'a shade better than the XK120, but with superior roadholding and braking, and a much smaller frontal area.' As the Porsche was fitted with the standard 356 wheels and 5.00 × 16in crossply tyres, Bentley's complimentary

The early Roadster was intended for the sunnier parts of North America, so the soft-top, little more than a sheet of cotton stretched over a simple frame, was rarely needed.

As the America Roadster was hand-built, each one differed in detail. The dashboard is quite different from the normal production version, lacking a glovebox lid, provision for a radio and the familiar hump in the middle.

The first Roadsters had just one air intake in the rear lid, like the production cars, but a second one was added on later versions.

Introduced in September 1954, the beautiful Speedster would never have come into being but for the American Porsche importer, Max Hoffman, pestering the factory for a more sporting alternative to the cabriolet. This is an early 1500, dating from the 'Pre-A' period. As the Speedster was intended to be an inexpensive Porsche, the soft-top did not have an inner lining. The frame should be painted beige.

observations on handling and roadholding make it difficult to imagine the manner in which the Jaguar went round corners...

As an aside, it is worth mentioning that after the Second World War the shortage of sports cars in Germany led a number of wealthy individuals to construct their own, usually with aluminium bodies fitted to Volkswagen chassis and utilising mildly tuned versions of the standard Beetle engine. By the early 1950s racing enthusiasts had switched to Porsche engines, and one such was Heinrich Sauter, a Stuttgart-based industrialist who built his own lightweight Roadster. Weighing 1325lb (600kg), it was lighter than Porsche's America Roadster

which, even in racing trim, tipped the scales at 1575lb (715kg). Sauter's Porsche Roadster was raced throughout 1951, though not successfully, after which it was sold to François Picard, who painted it 'French Blue' and raced it as 'Le Petit Tank'.

SPEEDSTER

Introduced in September 1954, the Speedster was created after Max Hoffman, Porsche's American agent, pestered the factory for a cheaper, more sport-ing version of the cabriolet. An Austrian, Hoffman knew the Porsche family well enough to express reservations about the styling of the regular 356, and

Substantially different inside from the normal production cars, the Speedster was fitted with hip-hugging bucket seats, a shroud over the instrument binnacle and lacked wind-up windows. Early Speedsters had two large instruments and a smaller one between the two, but after the introduction of the 356A all three gauges were of equal size with the tachometer in the middle and the speedometer to the right.

Ferry Porsche listened to his views with interest.

Hoffman wanted a cleaned-up version of the Roadster, a fun road car that could, if its owner wished, be taken to a racing circuit and used in competition. Ferry Porsche's scepticism about the number of cars Hoffman claimed would sell turned out to be right but in four years of production, with approximately 4854 cars built, the Speedster became the object of every boy racer's dream. Today, it is a cult car and a truly classic Porsche of immense desirability and with a certain exclusivity.

Beutler was responsible for constructing the Speedster's stunning bodywork, which clothed a standard chassis. Like the Roadster, it had a slightly hump-backed appearance but the doors did not have the ugly cutaways that made the Roadster look so odd, and the wheel arches were nothing like as crude. The curved flanks tapered steeply towards the ground at the rear and the overall 'slipperiness' of the shell gave it a most purposeful stance. Not that the Speedster's appearance was universally admired: with the hood down some said it resembled an inverted bathtub, and indeed there were heretics who even considered it ugly!

Compared with a cabriolet, the windscreen was much shorter and its chrome-plated brass frame was

This Speedster is a 1600 Super, dating from the 356A period and using the 75bhp engine.

With its low windscreen frame, rudimentary hood and different body styling, some likened the Speedster to an inverted bathtub and a few even called it ugly, but it is this model that enthusiasts today regard as the classic Porsche.

Gold-coloured Speedster script appears on the front wings, and, unlike on coupés and cabriolets, waistline trim was fitted to break up the bold flanks (above right). The chromed brass windscreen frame (far right) was shallower than the one fitted to the cabriolet. The detachable sidescreens and single-skin hood were never very effective in bad weather.

more rounded, and altogether prettier. The short windscreen certainly contributed to the Speedster's sporting appearance, but it was impractical for tall drivers: anyone over 5ft 9in would find himself staring straight into the top of the frame, the only remedy for this visibility problem being to snuggle lower in the seat so that, over long distances, a dull backache was the inevitable result.

Since the Speedster was largely intended for America's warmer climates, the soft-top was basic in the extreme and let in draughts at the best of times. A cotton top was stretched over a flimsy steel frame, there was no headlining and there were detachable

sidescreens instead of proper winding windows. As a result, the Speedster's doors were tailor-made for the car and are not interchangeable with other models. The 'Speedster' badges at the top of the front wings are gold-coloured and sit above 'waistline' trim which continues across the doors and rear wings.

The interior was fairly spartan. The seats were very different from those of the cabriolet and coupé, and reflected the car's sporting nature. Covered in leather or vinyl according to customer preference, they were of true bucket style, very hard to sit in and with generous side pieces for lateral support. The seat frame, normally steel, was aluminium on GT

versions, but those fitted to the early cars were fixed into position and could not be tilted forward. One of the most aesthetically appealing car seats ever made for a sports car, the Speedster style has been aped by after-market manufacturers to this day. Vinyl was used for the interior door panels, which were not fitted with map pockets. The later Convertible D and Roadster had a small, lockable storage bin on the driver's side. Speedsters were also without sun visors and door pulls, both of which were featured on the coupés and cabriolets. Surprisingly, Speedsters were fitted with carpeting, usually beige in colour and edged in vinyl. The carpet extended to the rear compartment, which was not fitted with seats in most examples.

The Speedster dashboard was also very different, its distinct, curved binnacle shrouding three main instruments, giving the car a most purposeful feel from behind the steering wheel. A horn ring for the steering wheel was an extra-cost option. The dashboard was painted body colour and there was no glovebox, only a lone Porsche 'flash' script and an angled grab handle appearing on the passenger's side. The top of the dashboard and the instrument shroud were neatly upholstered, a feature that endeared the car to so many enthusiasts. To begin with, the two main instruments – speedometer and tachometer –

The Speedster was superseded in August 1958 by the Convertible D, which had increased levels of comfort and a tall windscreen. Improvements included a larger back window for the soft-top.

Wind-up windows and a lockable door compartment, similar in appearance to a school satchel, are two features of the D's interior that distinguish it from the Speedster.

The Speedster's familiar shrouded instrument binnacle lived on. This layout, with three dials of equal size, had been adopted on the Speedster for the 1956 model year. The steering wheel, which had also been the standard fitting on later Speedsters, was more in keeping with the D's touring, rather than racing, image.

Unlike the Speedster, the D was not available with the Carrera power unit, and was offered with a choice of 60bhp and 75bhp engines only.

The Convertible D's 'bath-tub' styling was inherited from the Speedster, but purists, particularly in the US, thought the car had been softened.

Whereas the Speedster's low windscreen, though impractical, had looked right for a low-slung sports car, the full-height screen fitted to the D's body appeared ungainly. The Speedster's bucket seats were changed for more conventional cabriolet items.

flanked a smaller oil temperature gauge, but at the time of the 356A's introduction the three dials became the same size, and arguably looked better for it. A petrol gauge was introduced at the same time, and a clock was always optional. An ashtray was never fitted. Whereas cabriolet and coupé models had the ignition switch positioned on the left of the instrument cluster, the Speedster's was on the right. The hand throttle, which was placed at the base of the dashboard on the regular cars, was close to the ignition switch on the Speedster. A courtesy light never featured on the Speedster – but there was little to see in the interior anyway.

Originally fitted with the plain-bearing 1500, the 1300 Normal or 1300 Super engines, the Speedster also became available with two versions of the 1600 engine, the 60bhp Normal and 75bhp Super, upon the introduction of the 356A in 1955. The 75bhp Super was distinguished from the 60bhp Normal by its roller-bearing crankshaft, and along with its 'tin-top' and cabriolet sisters this version was affectionately nicknamed the 'Super 75'. Both versions of the 1300 engine were dropped in the spring of 1955. A GS road-going Carrera version fitted with the 1498cc (91.4cu in) four-cam engine was also introduced in 1955, and followed by a GT version, officially known as the GS GT, in 1957. More com-

The successor to both the Speedster and Convertible D, the spartan production Roadster was introduced in 1959. Initially it was built by Drauz, but production transferred to the Belgian coachbuilder and Porsche importer, D'Ieteren. The chromed 5½J wheels on this car are not the original fitting.

Like its austere predecessors, the Roadster's soft-top was unlined. Because the windscreen was taller, modifications had to be made to the frame.

monly referred to simply as the 'GT', it was intended primarily for racing and to that end was fitted with aluminium alloy doors and front and rear lids.

Like all Speedsters, the GT was aimed largely at the American market, and in 1957 carried a hefty price tag of $5305. However, the car was capable of accelerating from 0-60mph in 8.7sec and had a top speed in the region of 110-115mph, performance figures which justified the high price tag for the few lucky owners who could afford to buy and run one of these delectable racers. Fitted with twin Solex 40 PJI carburettors, the four-cam engine developed 100bhp at 6200rpm and maximum torque of 91lb ft at 5200rpm.

One important difference between the Carrera Speedster and the less exotic versions was that it used the 550 Spyder racing car's front brakes, which increased the overall brake lining area from 115sq in to 128sq in. Like the Spyder, the Speedster GT lacked a heater and was without underseal on the underside of the floorpan. At 1848lb (838kg), it was 140lb (63kg) lighter than the regular Speedsters.

On the whole, the Speedster remained virtually unchanged from the prototype to the last car made. The absurdly small hood was raised in height in 1957 and was given a larger rear window at the same time, but it was not enough. As far as sales were con-

cerned, the Speedster was a failure. The car was comparatively expensive, and customers who wanted a lightweight, sparsely-equipped sports car that could quickly be turned into an even more primitive racing car fell into a small minority. Porsche's profit margin was small and the car was dropped in 1958.

CONVERTIBLE D

However, not all was lost because the much-loved but slow-selling Speedster was immediately replaced by the Convertible D (the D standing for the car's

The Speedster's ancestry can still be traced in the dashboard, but the Roadster's seats were borrowed from the cabriolet and were considerably less shapely. Like the Convertible D, the Roadster also has a lockable compartment on the door panel.

All Speedsters, Convertible Ds and Roadsters were fitted with this style of Porsche dashboard script.

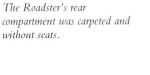

Like the Convertible D, the Roadster was not available as a Carrera and came with the usual choice of pushrod 1600 engines.

The Roadster's rear compartment was carpeted and without seats.

body builder, Drauz), a car that boasted a full-height windscreen, a proper hood and a less spartan interior. But Speedster addicts made their feelings about the later car known in no uncertain terms. A 'Speedster' with a luxurious hood and a more lavish interior was not a proper Speedster, and the factory lost no time in renaming the car the Roadster (after some further revisions) to avoid further upsetting this small band of fanatics.

A Carrera version of the Convertible D was not built, but after production of the Speedster came to an end in 1958 a short production run of 25 Carrera Speedsters was built in 1959 and fitted with the 1600

four-cam engine. All of these cars were to lightweight GT specification and were made for racing at the request of regular American customers.

ROADSTER

For the second time Porsche offered a 356 derivative called a Roadster, although the 1958 variety was a far cry from the original America Roadster. As Porsche's association with the Drauz concern ended in 1959, the Roadster bodies were built by the Belgian Porsche importer and coachbuilders Anciens Etablissement d'Iteren Frères S.A. in Brussels. Basically, the Roadster was a development of the Speedster and Convertible D, with a larger windscreen and back window, and larger side windows operated by conventional winders. The hood had a slightly revised frame to give more headroom but, like the Speedster hood, it did not have a lining.

Unlike the Speedster, the revised car was fitted with a cigarette lighter positioned next to the dashboard script, but an ashtray was only an option and there was still no interior light. The interior door panels were fitted with map pockets on both sides, and on the driver's side was a lockable compartment resembling a school satchel for storing odds and ends. The seats also differed: gone were the frugally

padded, beautifully sculpted Speedster seats and in their place were more conventional, generously padded seats with little lateral support.

The Roadster was a more practical car for everyday use, if only because it was possible to see out properly when the hood was raised. To the majority, however, it was not as handsome as the Speedster because the larger windscreen belonged more properly on the cabriolet body and looked just a little awkward. Whereas the Speedster was also available as a Carrera, the Roadster came with only the 60bhp or 75bhp engines. The model was dropped in 1962.

HARDTOPS

For 356 owners who wanted the best of both worlds, hardtops were available from the factory or from independent specialists, mostly in America. Whereas the Karmann hardtop model (see page 53) had its steel roof welded in place, the removable types were made out of glass-fibre. No-one really took to the Speedster's looks with the hood erected, but the detachable hardtop, with its smooth roof panel, was arguably an improvement. Cars fitted with plastic tops are a comparatively rare sight nowadays because the passage of time has done little to improve their popularity or desirability.

An essential piece of equipment for all convertibles. A tonneau cover (above) was never provided as standard, but was listed either as a factory option or an accessory. Like the Convertible D, the Roadster's soft-top (left) had a larger back window than the Speedster's, and there were wind-up windows in place of removeable sidescreens.

The attractive Drauz coach-builder's badge was fitted to the front wing.

BUYING & RESTORATION

When buying a Porsche it is best to assume the worst about its overall condition, irrespective of its shiny paintwork, retrimmed interior and apparently rebuilt mechanical components, because unfortunately there are as many badly restored cars in circulation as there are good ones. This is partly because in the days before the classic car boom of the late 1980s, the world had almost forgotten the 356. There was a hard core of enthusiasts who cared for them, naturally, but because prices were low major restoration work was not often viable. Some cars were neglected, others bodged to keep them running with inevitable consequences.

When investors started buying old cars to make money during the late 1980s the 'bodgers' had a field day, realising that even the shabbiest 356 could be made to look presentable after a couple of days spent with a welding torch, some well-aimed two-pack paint and a bucket of underseal. Stories about bodged cars are rife and anyone embarking on major restoration work should not be too surprised to find a complete nightmare beneath the pretty paintwork.

In view of the enormous cost of restoration work, the condition of the bodywork and the chassis should be the prime consideration. And beware of advertisements for the ubiquitous Californian car that is described as 'rust-free', because what that often means is that the rust *is* free, and there is plenty of it. During the 1950s and 1960s, few motor manufacturers took steps to proof their products against corrosion and Porsche was no exception. In those days it was not so necessary because the roads of Britain and Europe were not salted as much during the winter months. As a result, genuinely original rust-free Porsches are almost impossible to find.

When buying a car do not be in a hurry to part with your money, no matter how little the asking price. Talk to the owner: the conversation will soon reveal whether he or she is a true enthusiast who really cares about Porsches. Take a long look at every part of it: often a 356 that has been bodged to make a fast buck will have tell-tale signs that not all is well. It might only be small ripples in the body panels or a little overspray on the window rubbers but such features will need to be investigated carefully. After all, the 356 was not intended as a sedate shopping car and earlier examples may well have had more than one brush with the scenery, particularly in the hands of aspiring racing drivers.

In his book *Porsche 356* Denis Jenkinson says: 'On early cars tail-end damage was rife because so many owners had been caught out by the Porsche's inherent oversteering characteristics. In later years the scene changed to front-end damage, as cars understeered themselves into accidents, mainly because the drivers had not felt the limit being reached and had either put on more steering lock or braked, both of which would guarantee a forwards accident.' Unfortunately many of these badly damaged cars will have been repaired to a poor standard and are still on the road today.

So, try to discover whether the body is straight and true. Take measurements from front to rear on both sides of the car, measure the width at the front and rear and, most importantly, check the diagonal

A common site for severe rust is the area around the headlamps – the headlamp pods will have to be cut away and replaced. Sub-standard repairs with copious quantities of body filler here are common on badly restored Porsches.

The only way to determine the true state of the metalwork inside a 356 is to strip the cabin completely. Surface rust may be removed with a shotblaster, but it is obvious here that some new panelwork will be needed.

A previous repair such as this sill 'plate' on an otherwise unrestored car will often prove troublesome. It is best to be rid of it and start afresh.

measurements of the bodywork. Check the tyres for abnormal wear, which may result from a twisted or badly repaired chassis. The 'shutlines' of the doors, front lid and engine lid should be perfectly aligned with the bodywork at a distance of 3.5mm, and if there are wide gaps and a poor fit, be suspicious that the car has been involved in an accident, although it may be that the panels simply have not been refitted properly, a notoriously difficult job.

It is a good idea to pull back small sections of the window sealing rubbers with your finger nails, because perished rubbers will have allowed rain water to seep in, and rust is the inevitable consequence in these vulnerable areas. The roof pillars on coupé versions should also come in for the closest scrutiny, and although a small area of rust bubbling through the paintwork may be limited to surface corrosion as the result of a stone chipping hitting the body, it is just as likely to be serious corrosion working its way out from the inside. Because the easiest and cheapest way to disguise rust is to daub on copious quantities of plastic body filler, checks on these and other vulnerable areas can be made in the time-honoured fashion with a magnet.

As no part of the 356 is immune to corrosion, the bottoms of the doors, the sills, the front valance and the front and rear wings can all present a fairly sorry sight. Mud trapped on the underside of the wings will retain water and these panels can, if left unchecked, simply rot away. Particularly vulnerable are the vertical edges close to the front of the doors. Trapped rainwater can also rot the bottom of the headlamp pods but this area is difficult to check without actually removing the headlamps. If the car's owner objects to this, invite him to do it for you, and draw your own conclusions from a refusal to co-operate. Because the bodyshell contains so many mud and water traps it is vital to check every possible part. On the whole, open-top versions like Speedsters, Roadsters and Cabriolets tend to suffer more from rust because they are less weatherproof, the Speedster being the most vulnerable because of its rudimentary hood. The bright trim may well need to be replaced or refurbished, particularly on a car with brand new paintwork.

The electrically operated sunroof introduced on the T6 can also be a nightmare for restorers. Like the majority of sunroofs, the ones fitted to Porsches will in time corrode and leak water. Many things can go wrong with the motor itself, the flexible shaft attached to it and the attendant electrical cables, which very often develop kinks in them and simply wear out. Naturally, the removal of the electric motor for repair requires part of the headlining to be removed, a delicate operation in itself which, done inexpertly, can easily result in the need for a new headlining. In the worst cases, the sunroof cannot be opened with brute force and ignorance because of

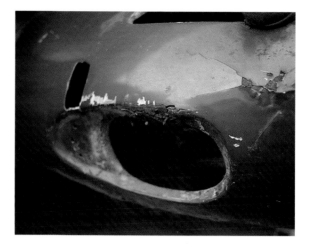

Here there are signs of accident damage as well as corrosion. Only by stripping off the paint will it become clear if a localised repair will suffice, or whether the front panel will have to be replaced.

The lower B-post and part of the sill area have completely rotted away, a sure sign that serious corrosion will have spread to the inner surfaces of both sections.

A series of small holes on the outer edge of the sill confirms that the entire sill needs replacing for the sake of the car's structural integrity.

rust. Bringing such a unit back to full health will test the patience of even the most persistent professional, but it can be done.

Under the front lid there is plenty of scope for rusting, especially in and around the spare wheel well and battery box. By surveying the metalwork closely it may even be possible to detect evidence of crash damage, which can often result in localised 'rippling' in parts of the front apron.

Inside the car, the condition of the driver's seat is

Perished window sealing rubbers let rainwater into the inner parts of the bodyshell. In this case restoration might not be economically viable.

Although the upper part of the lower A-post has escaped the ravages of corrosion, plenty of work is needed below. Again, this is a common site for advanced rust in a 356.

Corrosion is rarely a serious problem in the 356's engine bay, especially if it has been regularly splashed with oil.

important because if it is an original item and has sagged in the middle or to the sides, it will give a good indication of the car's true mileage. The back-rest reclining mechanism can be rendered inoperable on old, unrestored cars because the fixing screws tend to work loose and the metal inside the seat bends out of shape. The upholstery and headlining should be carefully checked as replacements are expensive and tricky to fit.

It is a good idea to discover the condition of the inside of the doors and quarter panels by removing the interior panels if you can, and to remove any rubber mats and check the floorpan. If there are carpets which have been firmly fixed to the pan, gently tap the whole area with your fist and listen for ominous crunching noises. Signs that the carpets have soaked up water will mean that the floorpan is probably riddled with rust and holes. It will soon become apparent if there is serious corrosion here, and the same applies to the sills.

The condition of the steering wheel, switchgear, instruments and all the other minor interior fittings which wear out with use is important because of the cost of replacing them. It is also worth remembering that even minor items stamped with a Porsche badge or part number are unlikely to be cheap.

The next step is to jack the car up, support it safely on good quality axle stands and inspect the underside. If you are a newcomer to the 356 fold, do not rely on intuition to reach any conclusions about the health of the floorpan and the chassis longitudinal members. There are several areas which are prone to serious corrosion and even experts can be fooled by botched repairs that have been smoothed over with masses of underseal. Rust most commonly attacks the jacking points and the longitudinal chassis members, any repairs to which are easily disguised with underseal. Irregularities on the surface will point to rust eruptions but in the case of a car that purports to have been restored, a photographic record can indicate whether the repair work has been carried out properly.

Mechanically, the 356 is strong and durable. Virtually all the components are over-engineered and will tolerate neglect and abuse for longer than the majority of cars. The reliability of the pushrod engine is legendary and a well-maintained unit will last well over 100,000 miles with sensible treatment. Because the engine was developed from the Beetle's, its few problems are similar. Oil notoriously leaks from the pushrod tubes: only a couple of teaspoons every few hundred miles, but the mess it creates on the underside of the engine is unsightly. If it is allowed to accumulate along with mud and road grime, the finned cylinder barrels, heads and crankcase will not have a chance to cool properly, resulting in a badly overheating engine. Oil can also leak from the oil cooler, and from the rocker cover gaskets, particularly after new ones have been fitted. It is also critical for the long-term health of the Porsche engine that none of the tinware surrounding the engine is missing, and that the rubber seal that sits between the tinware and the bodywork is in good condition. Without these vital components the engine will overheat badly, and ultimately could need a complete overhaul.

Turn the ignition key and the flat-four should burble into life instantly and quickly settle down to a steady idle. It may feel lumpy in cold, damp weather but it should not take more than a minute or so to smooth out. Blue smoke coming from the exhaust may be indicative of wear in the valvegear, and a deep rumbling sound is usually a signal of excessive wear in the crankshaft bearings, although this can be confused with a hole in the exhaust system. Blip the throttle a couple of times and the exhaust note should really make you want to enjoy driving the car.

Porsche gearboxes, with or without synchromesh, are among the best. Changing gear, whether up or down, should be so effortless that shifts go almost unnoticed. Possible problems include noisy, worn bearings, worn synchromesh, jumping out of gear (often the result of wear in the rubber mounting on the nose of the 'box), a growling clutch release bearing and play in the linkage caused by wear in the plastic bushing. A common complaint about the Porsche transmission years ago was that the clutch cable was prone to snapping, but generally 356 cables will last well if they are not abused. A properly adjusted cable should not require the driver to press the clutch pedal all the way to the floor, and indeed constantly doing so will shorten the life of the cable appreciably. It is also important when a new cable is fitted that it is greased well beforehand and inserted into the conduit several times before being tightened up. Almost all gearbox problems are best left to experts, who have the special tools required and years of experience. To have a 'box rebuilt professionally is not expensive but a secondhand replacement may be a better short term bet.

To discover the true health of the steering gearbox, king and link pins, shock absorbers, torsion bars and other vital chassis components, it is best to get behind the wheel and drive the car. Without exception, everything should feel taut and precise. Sloppiness in the steering, excessive body roll and spongy or badly adjusted brakes that pull the car to one side are all indicative of a car that requires work. All of these problems can be put right but it is important to bear in mind the cost.

Inevitably vulnerable to the wear and tear of everyday use, the wheels are not very easy to restore to a satisfactory standard. The rims and centres can be sand-blasted and a thorough job will usually get rid of rust even in serious cases of corrosion, but the

This outer door skin appears to be in good condition, but the top ledge and inner structure are so badly corroded that a replacement – an expensive item for a 356 – will have to be fitted.

The front inner wing structure in a well used example like this can give endless scope for an experienced welder to practise his craft, but this one, surprisingly, does not appear to be in bad shape.

Although they are immensely strong and durable, the main chassis rails must be in good condition because they are critical to the 356's structural safety, and major restoration work here is lengthy. Note the rear torsion bar protruding from its cylindrical housing.

deep crevice between the centre and the rim is a little more tricky. Even using the most powerful blasting equipment, corrosion in this area is unlikely to be eradicated completely and it can be a long and difficult task persevering with the original wheels. A good rust-inhibiting chemical may do the trick if the manufacturer's instructions are followed to the letter. The wheels can be re-painted or re-chromed at considerable expense but to see the rust in the rim

A once-bodged repair to an accident-damaged door has resulted in extraordinary butchery. The holes were drilled to receive a pulling tool in order to straighten out the metal.

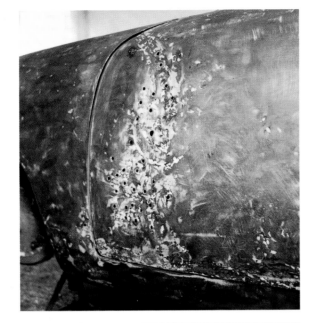

The impeccable quality of Porsche's original welding can just be seen at the point where the rear panel is joined to the wing.

Both repair panels fitted to this rear wing have been joined to the bodyshell with a MIG welder: the result, though adequate, is not as Dr Porsche originally intended.

return 12 months later is pretty demoralising, and it may be more cost-effective to invest in new wheels.

Nowadays, the 356 is exceptionally well catered for when it comes to spare parts. As more and more classic car enthusiasts have come to appreciate these wonderful little cars in recent years, a myriad of specialist companies, including Porsche itself, have gone out of their way to meet the needs of owners and would-be restorers, and it is now possible to build

almost any 356 back to its original factory specification. There are body panels for most cars and those that are not obtainable can be made. New engine parts and even secondhand bits and pieces are still available, although paying for them may be quite another matter. Reproduction parts are increasingly available too, including door handles, bright trim and window seals, but quality varies and will be reflected in the price.

The cost of restoring a 356 should not be underestimated, especially if the body and chassis are involved. Anyone who has been able to see a bodyshell that has been stripped of its paint will have a good idea of the engineering standard to which Porsche worked. The steel outer panels were gaswelded together, a notoriously difficult process which required years of training and practice. Gas welding produces tremendous heat which makes it impossible to avoid distorting each body panel when they are bonded together. Porsche's talented craftsmen were able to heat the metal and beat it perfectly into shape before it cooled – a highly skilled task. Many of these welds are so good that they are almost undetectable even where lead was not used to smooth out the joins. Luckily, there are still a few craftsmen able to practise gas welding. An alternative is to employ MIG welding techniques but the results, even in experienced hands, will rarely be as good. All too often astonishingly bad welding work is covered up with a plastic-based body filler, but this inadequate treatment certainly will not suffice for the discerning 356 owner.

It is worth paying careful attention to engine rebuilds. A 356 pushrod engine should be within the scope of a competent amateur mechanic with the right tools, a good workshop manual and a lot of patience. However, it is vital that the nuts and bolts holding everything together are undone and then done up in the factory-prescribed order. Failure to adhere rigidly to Porsche's instructions will certainly lead to problems, the very least of which will be severe oil leaks. Alternatively, a complete engine rebuild by a professional may be worth considering.

Rebuilding a four-cam engine should only be attempted by an acknowledged expert. Very few people fully understand how 'four-cammers' come apart, let alone how they go back together again, and they will be expensive. The sort of person who is capable of rebuilding a four-cam engine was probably able to construct a perfect replica of the Eifel Tower from match sticks while most of us were still wondering how to do up our shoe laces.

Restoring a Porsche cannot be accomplished in a hurry no matter how much money you have to spend or how many people you employ. Returning a car to its original condition could take many months, or even years. In some areas, it may be desirable to deviate from the original specification, for

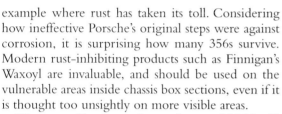

example where rust has taken its toll. Considering how ineffective Porsche's original steps were against corrosion, it is surprising how many 356s survive. Modern rust-inhibiting products such as Finnigan's Waxoyl are invaluable, and should be used on the vulnerable areas inside chassis box sections, even if it is thought too unsightly on more visible areas.

The cost of buying and restoring an old 356 will always be greater than the car's resulting market value and the prime reasons for embarking on such a task should be love and enthusiasm for Porsches. The idea of making money on such a project is not realistic. Joining a Porsche club and talking to experts is always a wise starting point, as those familiar with the 356 can offer good advice about the possible pitfalls. Many 'rogue' cars come up for sale regularly and some are known to the clubs.

If you do acquire a sound 356, whether it is in need of work or in concours condition, you will never look back. A 356 is a joy to own and drive.

The timeless shape of that gorgeous bodywork, the small air intakes on the engine lid, that famous squat stance, gleaming paintwork with just a scratch or two here and there that denotes the car has been used, and the knowledge that it was conceived by a family of undisputed brilliance, is worth all the hard work that must go into maintaining a 356.

Despite all the problems, the hard work you put into restoring your car will always be worthwhile. Naturally, there will be times when you will want to give up on the seemingly never-ending nature of the work. Merely sand-blasting a set of road wheels and painting them can take up to a week. Preparing the bodywork properly for painting can take months, especially if you are doing it in your spare time. And welding up a rusty chassis frame will almost undoubtedly give you food for thought if you started with the impression that plating the odd hole here and there would suffice. But never despair. Just keep going. Your efforts will bear rich fruit one day.

And after all the hard work has been completed, enjoy driving your 356 because that is what Dr Porsche intended it for. These 356As are pushrod cabriolet and Carrera coupé versions.

DATA SECTION

PRODUCTION CHANGES

1950

Distinguishing features of first 'Pre-A' model. Bodywork has distinctive 'V' shaped roof to accommodate 'split', two-piece windscreen, sills curve towards bottom and are without decorative trim, Porsche script on front panel, front lid fitted with solid handle without 'easy-grip' hole on underside, bumpers fitted closely to bodywork, engine lid has single air intake with decorative grille, front indicators inset on front panel but not directly below headlamps, rectangular tail lights with circular indicators above, brake light positioned in housing for number plate light, chromed Volkswagen hubcaps without familiar V-over-W emblem at their centres. Interior has wood door cappings, ivory coloured Volkswagen switchgear, steering wheel with three banks of four spokes, perspex sun visor on driver's side, cloth headlining, detachable dashboard, instruments are black faced with white numerals. Mechanically, the 356 relied heavily on Volkswagen components. The engine was a modified 1086cc 40bhp version of Volkswagen's air-cooled flat-four 25bhp unit. The steering, brakes and non-synchromesh gearbox were all VW.

Chassis numbers (1950): coupé and cabriolet 5001-5410.

1951
March

44bhp 1300 engine offered as an alternative to 1100 (which also remained in production), Veigel tachometer available as an alternative to a clock, finned alloy casing introduced on brake drums, twin-tone horns replace single-tone Volkswagen unit, remote oil temperature thermometer.

April

Telescopic shock absorbers replace lever-arm on rear suspension, opening rear side windows introduced.

October

Right-hand drive version introduced, mainly for British market.

Chassis numbers (1951): coupé and cabriolet 5132-5162, 5411-5600, 10001-10170, 10350-10432, 10531-11125.

1952
April

Single-piece windscreen replaces two-piece 'split' screen, but remains 'bent' in the middle, 10mm wide alloy windscreen trim fitted, tachometer standard but a clock is a special order alternative, fibreboard glovebox replaces steel, dashboard instruments have black faces and green numerals and are shrouded with hoods, front lid handle gains a hole on its underside for easier grip, wood door cappings replaced by painted metal (colour reflects interior trim and not body colour), lower 'B' post modified, toggle switch for indicators transferred from top of dashboard to steering column, ventilated road wheels replace solid type, rod linkage to carburettors from accelerator pedal replaces cable, rear seats lowered and folding backrests introduced to increase luggage space, tinted perspex sun visors fitted to both sides of the car as standard, improved sound insulation against engine noise.

May

Noise suppressors introduced on heater pipes.

June

Luggage compartment apron modified to accommodate battery further back and spare wheel at a more vertical angle to improve luggage space, bumpers moved away from bodywork and fitted with alloy mouldings with rubber inserts.

September

1500 55bhp plain-bearing engine introduced.

October

70bhp roller-bearing 1500S introduced, Porsche-designed synchromesh gearbox replaces Volkswagen gearbox, brake drums increased to 280mm diameter, gear lever cranked and relocated 120mm further forward, bumpers made wider and moved further away from body, valances modified correspondingly, twin round tail lights replace rectangular units (outer pair for indicators and tail lights, inner pair for brake lights), two-speed windscreen wipers available as an extra-cost option, leather strap replaces metal strap to secure spare wheel, front indicators mounted directly below headlamps instead of being inset on front panel, two-spoke VDM steering wheel replaces three-spoke wheel, Porsche crest on horn button.

Chassis numbers (1952): coupé 11126-12084, 50001-50098; cabriolet 10433-10469, 12301-12387, 15001-15116.

1953
October

60bhp roller-bearing 1300S introduced: first car's public launch at Paris Motor Show in October, deliveries to dealer showrooms from early November. Cabriolet's rear window made of clear plastic instead of glass.

Chassis numbers (1953): coupé 50099-51645; cabriolet 60001-60394.

1954
April

Pneumatically-operated fuel gauge introduced, seats re-shaped for improved comfort, steering wheel fitted with small 'segment' horn ring, steering wheel in a choice of colours (ivory, beige or grey), windscreen washers introduced with glass water reservoir, map pockets on interior door panels modified in shape, improved sound insulation for bodywork, horn grilles built into front indicators, grab handle fitted to passenger's side of dashboard, rheostat control for instrument lighting.

September

Speedster introduced in response to US demand for a more sporting version of the 356. Speedster differs from cabriolet in its 'bathtub' styling, unlined hood, side screens instead of wind-up windows, cut-down windscreen, bucket seats with lateral support and revised dashboard styling.

November

Long, pointed front lid handle with Porsche crest (similar to the one fitted to the Speedster) adopted across the range, engine crankcase made in three pieces instead of two, heater knob moved from dashboard to floor, glass bottle for windscreen washers changed for a plastic bag, front anti-roll bar fitted.

Chassis numbers (1954): coupé 51646-53008; cabriolet 60395-60722; Speedster 80001-80200.

1955
October

New 356A T1 introduced after public launch in September at Frankfurt Motor Show. 16in wheels replaced by 4½J × 15 wheels with 5.60 × 15 crossply tyres, modern curved windscreen replaces 'bent' screen, the roof line modified correspondingly, sills altered in shape and fitted with decorative alloy strip with rubber insert, interior modernised with perforated or 'spotted' vinyl headlining to replace cloth, full horn ring on steering wheel, dashboard instruments have built-in warning lights, single gearbox mounting replaced by two, 60bhp pushrod engine and four-cam 1500 100bhp Carrera engine introduced, rear shock absorbers repositioned vertically instead of at an angle, steering damper fitted.

Chassis numbers (1955): coupé 53009-55000; cabriolet 60723-61000; Speedster 80201-81900. From October for 1956 model year: coupé 55001-55390, cabriolet 61001-61069, Speedster 81901-82000.

An extra-cost option in its day, a Telefunken radio is now a delightful period piece. Streamlined wing mirrors were usually fitted to GT Carreras but were not exclusive to this model.

1956

July

US-style bumpers fitted with enlarged overriders and additional protective bar above main blade.

Chassis numbers (1956): coupé 55391-58311; cabriolet 61070-61499; Speedster 82001-82850.

1957

March

Twin circular tail lights replaced by single 'teardrop' type, front indicators fitted with large chromed surround, rear number plate light and reversing light placed below number plate, ashtray increased in size and placed beneath dashboard, padded sun visors replace tinted perspex items, cabriolet and Speedster rear windows enlarged.

September

Reworked T2 version of 356A launched at Frankfurt Motor Show, incorporating March 1957 modifications. Super model fitted with plain-bearing crankshaft, Zenith 32 NDIX carburettors for both Normal and Super variants, oil temperature sender unit repositioned on top of engine (instead of underneath), crankcase modified to improve oil flow, oil cooler enlarged and strengthened, tailpipes routed through bumper overriders to improve ground clearance, floorpan modified to accept seat belt anchorage points, higher geared window winders for easier operation, 'B' posts modified slightly in shape and latches moved further down pillars, door locks strengthened and external door handles curved at rear edge (instead of squared off), steering wheel increased in size by 25mm to 425mm, Porsche crest fitted to hubcaps (standard on Super, optional on Normal), quarterlights standard on cabriolet but optional on coupé, cabriolet's hood becomes removable so it can be changed for a hardtop (with corresponding changes to rear compartment), heater knob moved forward of gear lever.

Chassis numbers (1957): coupé 58312-59090; cabriolet 61500-61700; Speedster 82851-83691. From March: coupé 100001-101692; cabriolet 61701-61892. T2 from September: coupé 101693-102504; cabriolet 150001-150149; Speedster 83792-84366.

1958

August

Relatively unsuccessful Speedster dropped and Convertible D launched with rear window increased in size, wind-up windows instead of removeable sidescreens, standard cabriolet seats instead of bucket type, taller windscreen, windscreen washer.

Chassis numbers (1958): coupé 102505-106174; cabriolet 150150-151531; Speedster 84367-84922; Convertible D 85501-85886.

1959

September

356B T5 introduced at Frankfurt Motor Show, headlamps positioned higher with corresponding modifications to front wings, front and rear bumpers repositioned 95mm and 105mm higher on bodywork respectively, quarterlights fitted to door windows on coupé as standard, headroom in rear improved because split rear seats allow cushions to be lowered, new 'tulip' shaped three-spoked dished safety steering wheel with optional horn ring, steering wheel rim in black plastic as standard or wood as extra-cost option, dashboard switches and knobs in black plastic, indicators and headlamp flasher combined in switch positioned on steering column, shorter gear lever, demisting outlets either side of coupé's rear window, more powerful 90bhp version of 1600 pushrod engine available in addition to 60bhp and 75bhp engines, new Super 90 model fitted with rear compensating spring, new

IDENTIFICATION

Year	Dating notes	Engine size	Engine type	Engine numbers	Chassis numbers
356 Pre-A					
1950		1100	369	0101-0411	5001-5410
1951		1100	369	0412-0999	5132-5162
				10001-10137	5411-5600
				1001-1099	10001-10170
		1300	506	20001-20821	10350-10432
	From Oct	1500	527	30001-30737	10531-11125
1952		1100	369	10138-10151	10433-10469
		1300	506	20822-21297	11126-12084
	To Sep	1500	527	30738-30750	12301-12387
	From Sep	1500	546	30751-31025	50001-50098
	From Oct	1500S	528	40001-40117	15001-15116
1953		1100	369	10152-10161	Coupé 50099-51645
		1300	506	21298-21636	Cabriolet 60001-60394
		1500	546	31026-32569	
		1500S	528	40118-40685	
	From Nov	1300S	589	50001-50017	
1954		1100	369	10162-10199	Coupé 51646-53008
		1300	506	21637-21780	Cabriolet 60395-60722
	To May	1300S	589	50018-50099	Speedster 80001-80200
	Jun to Nov	1300A	506/1	21781-21999	
	To Nov	1500	546	32570-33899	
	To Nov	1500S	528	40686-40999	
	From Nov	1300	506/2	22001-22021	
	From Nov	1300S	589/2	50101-	
	From Nov	1500	546/2	33901-34119	
	From Nov	1500S	528/2	41001-41048	
1955	To Oct	1300	506/2	22022-22245	Coupé 53009-55000
	To Oct	1300S	589/2	-50127	Cabriolet 60723-6200
	To Oct	1500	546/2	34120-35790	Speedster 80201-81900
	To Oct	1500S	528/2	41049-41000	
356A					
1955		1300	506/2	22246-222273	Coupé 55001-55390
		1300S	589/2	50128-50135	Cabriolet 61001-61069
		1600	616/1	60001-60608	Speedster 81901-82000
		1600S	616/2	80001-80110	
1956		1300	506/2	22274-22471	Coupé 55391-58311
		1300S	589/2	50136-50155	Cabriolet 61070-61499
		1600	616/1	60609-63926	Speedster 82001-82850
		1600S	616/2	80111-80756	
1957	To Sep	1300	506/2	22472-22999	To Mar: Coupé 58312-59090
	To Sep	1300S	589/2	50156-50999	Cabriolet 61500-61700
	To Sep	1600	616/1	63927-66999	Speedster 82851-83691
	To Sep	1600S	616/2	80757-81199	From Mar: Coupé 100001-101692
					Cabriolet 61701-61892
	From Sep	1600	616/1	67001-68216	Coupé 101693-102504
	From Sep	1600S	616/2	81201-81521	Cabriolet 150001-150149
					Speedster 83792-84366
1958		1600	616/1	68217-72468	Coupé 102505-106174
		1600S	616/2	81522-83145	Cabriolet 150150-151531
					Speedster 84367-84922
					Convertible D 85501-85886

IDENTIFICATION

Year	Dating notes	Engine size	Engine type	Engine numbers	Chassis numbers
356A continued					
1959	To Sep	1600	616/1	72469-79999	Coupé 106175-108917
	To Sep	1600S	616/2	83146-84770	Cabriolet 151532-152475
					Convertible D 85887-86830
356B					
1959	From Sep	1600	616/1	600101-601500	Coupé 108918-110237
	From Sep	1600S	616/2	84771-85550	Cabriolet 152476-152943
					Roadster 86831-87391
1960		1600	616/1	601501-604700	Coupé 110238-114650
		1600S	616/2	85551-88320	Cabriolet 152944-154560
		1600 S-90	616/7	800101-802000	Roadster 87392-88920
1961	To Sep	1600	616/1	604701-606799	Coupé 114651-117476
				88321-89999	Karmann Hardtop 200001-201048
	To Sep	1600S	616/2	085001-085670	Cabriolet 154561-155569
	To Sep	1600 S-90	616/7	802001-803999	Roadster 88921-89483
	From Sep	1600	616/1	606801-607750	Coupé 117601-118950
	From Sep	1600S	616/12	700001-701200	Karmann Hardtop 201601-202200
	From Sep	1600 S-90	616/7	804001-804630	Cabriolet 155601-156200
					Roadster 89601-89800
1962	To Jul	1600	616/1	607751-608900	Coupé 118951-121099
	To Jul	1600S	616/12	701201-702800	Karmann Hardtop 202201-202299
		1600 S-90	616/7	804631-805600	Karmann Coupé 210001-210899
					Cabriolet 156201-156999
	From Jul	1600	616/1	608901-61000	Coupé 121100-123042
	From Jul	1600S	616/12	702801-705050	Karmann Coupé 210900-212171
	From Jul	1600 S-90	616/7	805601-806600	Cabriolet 157000-157768
1963	To Jul	1600	616/1	610001-611000	
				0600501-0600600	
				611001-611200	
	To Jul	1600S	616/12	705051-706000	Coupé 132304-125239
				0700501-07011200	Karmann Coupé 212172-214400
				706001-707200	Cabriolet 157769-158700
	To Jul	1600 S-90	616/7	806601-807000	
				0800501-0801000	
				807001-807400	
356C					
1963	From Jul	1600C	616/15	710001-711870	Coupé 126001-128104
				730001-731102	Karmann Coupé 215001-216738
	From Jul	1600SC	616/16	810001-811001	Cabriolet 159001-159832
				820001-820522	
1964		1600C	616/15	711871-716804	Coupé 128105-131927
				731103-733027	Karmann Coupé 216739-221482
		1600SC	616/16	811002-813562	Cabriolet 159833-161577
				820523-821701	
1965		1600C	616/15	716805 onwards	Coupé 138928 onwards
				733028 onwards	Karmann Coupé 221483 onwards
		1600SC	616/16	813563 onwards	Cabriolet 161578 onwards
				821702 onwards	

Roadster model introduced to replace Convertible D.
Chassis numbers (1959): coupé 106175-108917; cabriolet 151532-152475; convertible 85887-86830. 356B T5 from September: coupé 108918-110237; cabriolet 152476-152943; Roadster 86831-87391.

1960
August
Karmann-built hardtop coupé introduced, distinctive hardtop welded to cabriolet bodyshell.

Chassis numbers (1960); coupé 110238-114650; cabriolet 152944-154560; Roadster 87392-88920.

1961
September
'Facelifted' T6 version of the 356B introduced, front lid enlarged and floor of luggage compartment fitted with plastic liner, engine lid enlarged and single air intake replaced by two, coupé windscreen and rear window enlarged, optional sunroof electrically operated (not manually), redesigned luggage compartment includes fusebox behind dashboard on left-hand side, battery positioned asymmetrically on right, spare wheel mounted flatter, available luggage space increased due to flatter fuel tank and filler neck directed to the right-hand front wing (on left-hand drive cars only), windscreen wiper motor increased in power to 60 watts and two-speed action changed for 'infinitely' variable rheostat, air intake louvres introduced on front scuttle below windscreen to improve cabin ventilation, electrically-operated clock standard, rear-view mirror with switchable 'anti-dazzle' facility, zipper fitted to cabriolet's hood to allow for removal of rear window, diameter of clutch plate increased from 180mm to 200mm on 90bhp model, Carrera 2 with 130bhp 2-litre four-cam engine introduced.

Chassis numbers (1961): coupé 114651-117476; Karmann Hardtop 200001-201048; cabriolet 154561-155569, Roadster 88921-89483. From September (356B T6): coupé 117601-118950; Karmann Hardtop 201601-202200; cabriolet 155601-156200; Roadster 89601-89800.

1962
June
Roadster and Karmann hardtop versions dropped due to poor sales.

Chassis numbers (1962): coupé 118951-121099; Karmann Hardtop 202201-202299; Karmann coupé 210001-210899; cabriolet 156201-156999. From July: coupé 121100-123042; Karmann coupé 210900-212171; cabriolet 157000-157768.

1963
July
The 356C introduced with ATE disc brakes on all four wheels, wheels and hubs modified accordingly and hubcaps flattened, engine choice confined to 75bhp and 95bhp pushrod units and 2-litre four-cam in Carrera version, pushrod-engined cars distinguished externally by 'C' tail script on 75bhp model and 'SC' on 95bhp car, rear compensating spring available only to special order, front anti-roll bar increased in diameter by 1mm, thick rubber Guibo coupling fitted to steering column to replace previous Volkswagen-style disc, handbrake warning light incorporated into combination gauge, modified vents on coupé for improved rear window demisting, magnetic glovebox lock introduced, seats redesigned for greater comfort, where leather not specified seats covered in improved leatherette, armrests fitted to interior panels of both doors, passenger grab handle covered in plastic, two zippers fitted to rear of cabriolet hood instead of one.

Chassis numbers (1963): coupé 132304-125239; Karmann coupé 212172-214400; cabriolet 157769-158700. 356C from July: coupé 126001-128104; Karmann coupé 215001-

216738; cabriolet 159001-159832.

Chassis numbers (1964): coupé 128105-131927, 216739-221482; cabriolet 159833-161577.

Chassis numbers (1965): coupé 138928 etc; Karmann coupé 221483 etc; cabriolet 161578 etc.

Note
Porsche records from the 356 period are insufficiently detailed to allow production changes reliably to be pinpointed by chassis number.

OPTIONS & ACCESSORIES

In the early 1950s, car radios were still a novelty and few of Porsche's customers were prepared to do without one. As radios were always optional extras they were mostly fitted by dealers. Expensive collectors' pieces today, the vast majority of radios supplied for the 356 were made by Blaupunkt, although a fair proportion of them were made by Telefunken in the early days.

The good old Blaupunkts, with their wonderful push buttons and simple illuminated dials, are some of the most enduring and reliable pieces of electrical equipment ever constructed but the fact that they can only receive long and medium wavebands limits their use today.

When the T2 356A was introduced in 1958, Porsche offered the option of an Eberspächer auxiliary heater to support the conventional heater that worked off the exhaust system. The Eberspächer was an expensive luxury, a complex unit utilising petrol from the car's main fuel system which it then burned to produce extra heat inside the cabin. Over the years these items have sometimes proved to be extremely unreliable, to the extent that a friend quite without shame once remarked that he had removed the one fitted to his car and buried it.

For those who found luggage space too limited, a luggage rack could be fitted to the engine lid. Large steel-frame structures designed to take a couple of suitcases, the majority were chrome-plated and supplied as accessories rather than official factory options. Leather ski straps were available at extra cost, the skis themselves fitting on either side of the luggage rack.

Spotlights were always popular accessories, particularly in Britain and Europe, and most were made by Bosch and Hella. External rear view mirrors of various types could be attached either to the doors or the front wings. Fitted as standard equipment in the late 1950s, all the dealer-supplied items required holes drilled in the bodywork before they could be attached, because of the design of the body.

A clock was available to order, as were two-speed windscreen wipers from October 1952. As a fuel gauge was not fitted until spring 1954, an 'after-market' one was available and proved a useful alternative to Porsche's rather inconvenient system of dipping the tank with a wooden stick.

Unlike the Beetle, the 356 did not lend itself particularly well to 'add-on goodies' and sticky bits and pieces, and most Porsche owners thought that superfluous gadgets were unnecessary. In North America, whitewall tyres found some favour.

The dozens of accessories made by the German Kamei company such as front and rear parcel shelves, footrests and additional ashtrays were primarily intended for Beetles, although some could undoubtedly be fitted to Porsches.

Retrospectively fitting accessories is very much a personal thing. There are devoted collectors of Porsche automobilia who will happily travel the world looking for every accessory capable of being fitted to a 356, and who will pay dearly for a 'complete set', but only the reader can choose whether to leave his or her car unadorned or to dress it up to look like a fortune teller's tent.

COLOUR SCHEMES

1951/52/53 Model Years (356)

Body colours
Black, Ivory, Strawberry Red, Pascha Red, Azure Blue, Adria Blue, Maroon, Fish Silver Grey, Medium Grey, Sand Grey, Radium Green, Palm Green.
Upholstery
Black, Blue, Red, Green, Yellow, Light Grey, Beige, Beige/Rose.
Note: It is not possible to identify precise paint/upholstery combinations from Porsche records.

1954/55 Model Years (356)

Body colour	COUPÉ Upholstery	CABRIOLET Upholstery	Hood	Tonneau
Black	Red	Red	Beige	Red
		Beige	Beige	Beige
	Beige with corduroy inserts	Green	Beige	Green
Metallic Silver	Red or Green	Red	Black	Red
	Red with corduroy inserts			
Metallic Graphite	Beige with corduroy inserts	Beige	Beige	Beige
	Yellow			
Turkish Red	Beige with corduroy inserts	Beige Rose	Beige Rose	Beige
	Yellow			
Terra Cotta		Yellow Earth	Beige	Yellow
Metallic Jade Green	Yellow with corduroy inserts	Beige	Grey Green	Beige
	Yellow			
Pearl Grey	Red	Blue	Grey Blue	Blue
	Blue with corduroy inserts			
Metallic Adria Blue	Red or Blue			
	Grey with corduroy inserts			
Ivory	Green with corduroy inserts			
	Green or Red			

1955 Model Year (356 Speedster only)

Body colour	Upholstery	Hood
White	Black, Red	Black
Speedster Blue	Cream, Tan	Tan
Signal Red	Cream, Tan	Tan
Fire Red	Black	Black

1956/57/58 Model Years (356A)

Body colour	COUPÉ Upholstery	CABRIOLET Upholstery	Dashboard	SPEEDSTER Upholstery	Hood
Black	Red, Red with Red corduroy	Red	Red	Red	Beige
	Beige, Beige with Beige corduroy		Beige	Black	
Metallic Silver	Red, Red with Red corduroy	Red	Red	Red	Black
	Green, Green with Green corduroy	Green	Green		
Ivory	Red, Red with Red corduroy	Red	Red	Red	Black
	Brown, Brown with Brown corduroy	Green	Green	Black	Black
Ruby Red	Brown, Brown with Brown corduroy	Beige	Red	Tan	Black
	Beige, Beige with Beige corduroy	Brown	Red	Black	Black
Fjord Green	Beige, Beige with Beige corduroy	Beige	Brown	Brown	Beige
	Brown, Brown with Brown corduroy	Beige	Brown		
Metallic Aquamarine	Red, Red with Red corduroy	Red	Red	Red	Black
	Brown, Brown with Brown corduroy	Brown	Brown		
Meissen Blue	Red, Red with Red corduroy	Red	Red	Red	Black
	Brown, Brown with Brown corduroy	Brown	Brown	Black	Black
Glacier White*	Brown, Brown with Brown corduroy	Black	Brown	Brown	Black
	Green, Green with Green corduroy	Green	Green	Black	Black
Stone Grey*	Brown, Brown with brown corduroy	Red	Red	Red	Black
	Red, Red with Red corduroy	Brown	Brown		
Auratium Green*	Beige, Beige with Beige corduroy	Beige	Brown	Beige	Beige
	Brown, Brown with Brown corduroy	Beige	Brown		
Orange*	Black	Black	Brown	Light Brown	Black
	Beige, Beige with Beige corduroy	Black	Black		

* Special paints

1959/60/61 Model Years (356A/B)

Body colour	COUPÉ Upholstery	CABRIOLET AND ROADSTER Upholstery
Ivory	Red, Red with Bordeaux corduroy	Red
	Black, Black with Mouse corduroy	Black
Ruby Red	Light Brown, Light Brown with Birch corduroy	Light Brown
	Light Grey, Light Grey with Stone corduroy	Light Grey
Metallic Silver	Red, Red with Bordeaux corduroy	Red
	Blue, Blue with Pearl corduroy	Blue
Slate Grey	Red, Red with Bordeaux corduroy	Red
	Light Grey, Light Grey with Stone corduroy	Light Grey
Aetna Blue	Red, Red with Bordeaux corduroy	Red
	Light Grey, Light Grey with Stone corduroy	Light Grey
Heron Grey	Red, Red with Bordeaux corduroy	Red
	Blue, Blue with Pearl corduroy	Blue
Fjord Green	Light Brown, Light Brown with Birch corduroy	Light Brown
	Light Grey, Light Grey with Stone corduroy	Light Grey
Black*	Red, Red with Bordeaux corduroy	Red
	Light Brown, Light Brown with Birch corduroy	Light Brown
Signal Red*	Black, Black with Mouse corduroy	Black
	Light Grey, Light Grey with Stone corduroy	Light Grey
Condor Yellow*	Black, Black with Mouse corduroy	Black
	Dark Grey, Dark Grey with Stone corduroy	Dark Grey
Royal Blue*	Black, Black with Mouse corduroy	Black
	Light Grey, Light Grey with Stone corduroy	Light Grey

1962/63 Model Years (356B)

Metallic Silver	Red, Red with Red corduroy	Red
	Blue, Blue Pearl Grey corduroy	Blue
Ruby Red	Black, Black with Mouse Grey corduroy	Black
	Grey, Grey with Pearl Grey corduroy	Grey
Ivory	Brown, Brown with Brown corduroy	Brown
	Red, Red with Red corduroy	Red
Slate Grey	Red, Red with Red corduroy	Red
	Green, Green with Green corduroy	Green
Heron Grey	Green, Green with Green corduroy	Green
	Brown, Brown with Brown corduroy	Brown
Champagne Yellow	Green, Green with Green corduroy	Green
	Black, Black with Mouse Grey corduroy	Black
Oslo Blue	Red, Red with Red corduroy	Red
	Grey, Grey with Pearl Grey corduroy	Grey
Black*	Red, Red with Red corduroy	Red
	Green, Green with Green corduroy	Green
Signal Red*	Black, Black with Mouse Grey corduroy	Black
	Grey, Grey with Pearl Grey corduroy	Grey
Bali Blue*	Light Brown, Light Brown with Light Brown corduroy	Light Brown
	Grey, Grey with Pearl Grey corduroy	Grey
Smyrna Green*	Brown, Brown with Brown corduroy	Brown
	Grey, Grey with Pearl Grey corduroy	Grey

1964/65 Model Years (356C)

Light Ivory	Red, Red with Red corduroy	Red
	Black, Black with Mouse Grey corduroy	Black
Ruby Red	Black, Black with Mouse Grey corduroy	Black
	Grey, Grey with Pearl Grey corduroy	Grey
Signal Red	Black, Black with Mouse Grey corduroy	Black
	Grey, Grey with Pearl Grey corduroy	Grey
Slate Grey	Red, Red with Red corduroy	Red
	Fawn, Fawn with Fawn corduroy	Fawn
Champagne Yellow	Green, Green with Green corduroy	Green
	Black, Black with Mouse Grey corduroy	Black
Sky Blue	Red, Red with Red corduroy	Red
	Fawn, Fawn with Fawn corduroy	Fawn
Irish Green	Fawn, Fawn with Fawn corduroy	Fawn
	Grey, Grey with Pearl Grey corduroy	Grey
Black*	Red, Red with Red corduroy	Red
	Green, Green with Green corduroy	Green
Togo Brown*	Green, Green with Green corduroy	Green
	Fawn, Fawn with Fawn corduroy	Fawn
Bali Blue*	Fawn, Fawn with Fawn corduroy	Fawn
	Grey, Grey with Pearl Grey corduroy	Grey
Dolphin Grey*	Blue, Blue with Pearl Grey corduroy	Blue
	Green, Green with Green corduroy	Green

* Special paints

PRODUCTION FIGURES

1948 1 mid-engined open-top prototype.

1949 49 alloy-bodied cars built at Gmünd, to 1951

1950 Production starts at Stuttgart, 298 coupés.

1951 900 coupés, 169 cabriolets.

1952 1057 coupés, 240 cabriolets.

1953 1547 coupés, 394 cabriolets.

1954 1363 coupés, 328 cabriolets, 200 Drauz-bodied Speedsters.

1955 Pre-A series cars: 1992 coupés, 278 cabriolets, 1700 Speedsters.
A-series cars: 390 coupés, 69 cabriolets, 100 Speedsters.

1956 2921 coupés, 430 cabriolets, 850 Speedsters.

1957 T1: 2471 coupés, 393 cabriolets, 841 Speedsters.
T2: 812 coupés, 149 cabriolets, 575 Speedsters.

1958 3670 coupés, 1382 cabriolets, 556 Speedsters, 386 Convertible Ds.

1959 T2: 2743 coupés, 944 cabriolets, 25 or 32 Speedsters, 944 Convertible Ds.
356B T5: 1320 coupés, 468 cabriolets, 561 Roadsters.

1960 4413 coupés, 1617 cabriolets, 1529 Roadsters.

1961 T5: 2826 coupés, 1009 cabriolets, 563 Roadsters, 1048 Karmann-built Hardtops.
T6: 1350 coupés, 600 cabriolets, 200 Roadsters, 600 Karmann-built Hardtops.

1962 6362 coupés, 1568 cabriolets. Of the coupés, 4092 were built by Reutter, 2171 by Karmann, and 99 Hardtops also by Karmann.

1963 T6: 4426 coupés, 932 cabriolets. Of the T6 coupés, 2197 were built by Reutter and 2229 by Karmann.
356C: 3842 coupés, 932 cabriolets. Of the 356C coupés, 2104 were built by Reutter and 1738 by Karmann.

1964 8567 coupés, 1745 cabriolets. Of the coupés, 3823 were built by Reutter and 4744 by Karmann.

1965 1100 coupés, 588 cabriolets. Of the coupés, 3 were built by Reutter and 1097 by Karmann.

1966 10 coupés were built and painted white for the Dutch police force to special order.

Total 356 'Pre-A'	10466
Total 356A T1	8465
Total 356A T2	12193
Total 356B T5	15354
Total 356B T6	16038
Total 356C	16684
Grand total	79200

Note
It is not possible to isolate production figures for Carrera models.

PUSHROD ENGINE SPECIFICATIONS

Technical data	1100 (369)	1300 (369)	1300A (506/1)	1300S (589)	1500 (527)	1500 (546)	1500S (528)	1300 (506/2)	1300S (589/2)
Years made	1950-54	1951-Jun 1954	Jun 1954-Nov 1954	Nov 1953-May 1954	Oct 1951-Sep 1952	Sep 1952-Nov 1954	Sep 1952-Nov 1954	Nov 1954-Sep 1957	Nov 1954-Oct 1955
Bore	73.5mm	80mm	74.5mm	74.5mm	80mm	80mm	80mm	74.5mm	74.5mm
Stroke	64mm	64mm	74mm	74mm	74mm	74mm	74mm	74mm	74mm
Cubic capacity	1086cc	1286cc	1290cc	1290cc	1488cc	1488cc	1488cc	1290cc	1290cc
Carburettors	32 PBI	32 PBI	32 PBI	32 PBI	40 PBIC	32 PBI	40 PBIC	32 PBI	32 PBIC
Compression ratio	7:1	6.5:1	6.5:1	8.2:1	7:1	7:1	8.2:1	6.5:1	8.2:1
Max power (DIN bhp)	40 at 4200rpm	44 at 4200rpm	44 at 4200rpm	60 at 5500rpm	60 at 5000rpm	55 at 4400rpm	70 at 5000rpm	44 at 4200rpm	60 at 5500rpm
Max torque (Mkp)	7.15 at 2800rpm	8.25 at 2800rpm	8.25 at 2800rpm	9.00 at 3600rpm	10.4 at 3000rpm	10.8 at 2800rpm	11.0 at 3600rpm	8.25 at 3800rpm	9.0 at 3600rpm
Mean piston speed (m/sec)	8.95	10.3	10.3	12.3	11.5	10.9	12.3	10.3	12.3
Crankshaft	Forged	Forged	Forged	Built-up	Built-up	Forged	Built-up	Forged	Built-up
Bearings 1, 2, 3	50mm	50mm	50mm	50mm	50mm	50mm	50mm	50mm	50mm
Bearing 4	40mm	40mm	40mm	40mm	40mm	40mm	40mm	40mm	40mm
Connecting rod bearings	50mm	50mm	53mm	Roller bearings	Roller bearings	53mm	Roller bearings	53mm	Roller bearings
Crankcase	2-piece	2-piece	2-piece	2-piece	2-piece	2-piece	2-piece	3-piece	3-piece
Valve timing									
Intake opens (BTDC)	2° 30′	2° 30′	2° 30′	19°	2° 30′	2° 30′	19°	2° 30′	19°
Intake closes (ABDC)	37° 30′	37° 30′	37° 30′	54°	37° 30′	37° 30′	54°	37° 30′	54°
Exhaust opens (BBDC)	37° 30′	37° 30′	37° 30′	54°	37° 30′	37° 30′	54°	37° 30′	54°
Exhaust closes (ATDC)	2° 30′	2° 30′	2° 30′	19°	2° 30′	2° 30′	19°	2° 30′	19°
Valve lift intake	8.5mm	8.5mm	8.5mm	9.6mm	8.5mm	8.5mm	9.6mm	8.5mm	9.6mm
Valve lift exhaust	8.2mm	8.2mm	8.2mm	9.25mm	8.2mm	8.2mm	9.25mm	8.2mm	9.25mm

American specification bumpers with an additional bar running through the overriders were introduced on the 356A. A full-width item on the early cars, the design was modified in 1956 to become two smaller bars, as seen here. Protective headlamp grilles were available as an extra-cost option from 1955.

PUSHROD ENGINE SPECIFICATIONS

Technical data	1500 (546/2)	1500S (528/2)	1600 (616/1)	1600S (616/2)	1600S (616/12)	1600 S90 (616/7)	1600C (616/15)	1600SC (616/16)
Years made	Nov 1954-Oct 1955	Nov 1954-Oct 1955	Oct 1955-Sep 1957	Oct 1955-Sep 1957	Sep 1961-Jul 1963	Sep 1961-Jul 1963	Jul 1963-Apr 1965	Jul 1963-Apr 1965
Bore	80mm	80mm	82.5mm	82.5mm	82.5mm	82.5mm	82.5mm	82.5mm
Stroke	74mm	74mm	74mm	74mm	74mm	74mm	74mm	74mm
Cubic capacity	1488cc	1488cc	1582cc	1582cc	1582cc	1582cc	1582cc	1582cc
Carburettors	32 PBI	40 PICB	32 PBIC	40 PICB	32 NDIX	40 PII-4	32 NDIX	40 PII-4
Compression ratio	7:1	8.2:1	7.5:1	8.5:1	8.5:1	9:1	8.5:1	9.5:1
Max power (DIN bhp)	55 at 4400rpm	70 at 5000rpm	60 at 4500rpm	75 at 5000rpm	75 at 5000rpm	90 at 5500rpm	75 at 5200rpm	95 at 5800rpm
Max torque (Mkp)	10.8 at 2800rpm	11.0 at 3600rpm	11.2 at 2800rpm	11.9 at 3700rpm	11.9 at 3700rpm	12.3 at 4300rpm	12.5 at 3600rpm	12.6 at 4200rpm
Mean piston speed (m/sec)	10.9	12.3	11.1	12.3	12.3	13.6	12.8	14.3
Crankshaft	Forged	Built-up	Forged	Forged	Forged	Forged	Forged	Forged
Bearings 1, 2, 3	50mm	50mm	50mm	50mm	50mm	55mm	50mm	50mm
Bearing 4	40mm	40mm	40mm	40mm	50mm	55mm	55mm	55mm
Connecting rod bearings	53mm	Roller bearings	53mm	53mm	53mm	53mm	53 mm	53 mm
Crankcase	3-piece	3-piece	3-piece	3-piece	3-piece	3-piece	3-piece	3-piece
Valve timing								
Intake opens (BTDC)	2° 30′	19°	7°	17°	17°	17°	10°	17°
Intake closes (ABDC)	37° 30′	54°	45°	53°	53°	53°	44°	53°
Exhaust opens (BBDC)	37° 30′	54°	44°	50°	50°	50°	42°	50°
Exhaust closes (ATDC)	2° 30′	19°	6°	14°	14°	14°	6°	14°
Valve lift intake	8.5mm	9.6mm	8.5mm	9.6mm	10.8mm	10.8mm	10.0mm	10.8mm
Valve lift exhaust	8.2mm	9.25mm	8.2mm	9.25mm	9.2mm	9.2mm	8.6mm	9.2mm

FOUR-CAM ENGINE SPECIFICATIONS

Technical data	1500GS (547/1)	1500GT (547/1)	1600GS (692)	1600GT (692)	Carrera 2 (587)	2000GS (587/2)	2000GT (587/2)
Years made	1955-58	1955-58	1958-59	1959-61	1962-64	1962-64	1962-64
Bore	85mm	85mm	87.5mm	87.5mm	92mm	92mm	92mm
Stroke	66mm	66mm	66mm	66mm	74mm	74mm	74mm
Cubic Capacity	1498cc	1498cc	1587.5cc	1587.5cc	1966cc	1966cc	1966cc
Carburettors	Solex 40 PJJ-4	Solex 40 PJJ-4	Solex 40 PJJ-4	Weber 40 DCM	Solex 40 PII-4	Weber 46 JDM	Weber 46 JDM
Compression ratio	9.0:1	9.0:1	9.0:1	9.8:1	9.5:1	9.8:1	9.8:1
Max power (DIN bhp)	100 at 6200rpm	100 at 6400rpm	105 at 6500rpm	115 at 6500rpm	130 at 6200rpm	140 at 6200rpm	155 at 6600rpm
Max torque (lb ft)	87 at 5200rpm	91 at 5200rpm	88 at 5000rpm	99 at 5500rpm	119 at 4600rpm	128 at 4700rpm	144 at 5600rpm
Mean piston speed (m/sec)	n/a	n/a	n/a	n/a	n/a	n/a	n/a
Crankshaft	Built-up	Built-up	Forged	Forged	Forged	Forged	Forged
Bearings 1, 2, 3	52mm	52mm	52mm	55mm	60mm	60mm	60mm
Bearing 4	52mm	52mm	52mm	55mm	60mm	60mm	60mm
Connecting rod bearings	52mm	52mm	52mm	55mm	52mm	52mm	52mm
Crankcase	2-piece	2-piece	2-piece	2-piece	2-piece	2-piece	2-piece
Valve timing							
Intake opens (BBDC)	77.5°	77.5°	77.5°	77.5°	77.5°	77.5°	77.5°
Intake closes (ATDC)	37.3°	37.3°	37.3°	37.3°	37.3°	37.3°	37.3°
Exhaust opens (BTDC)	37.5°	37.5°	37.5°	37.5°	37.5°	37.5°	37.5°
Exhaust closes (ABDC)	77.5°	77.5°	77.5°	77.5°	77.5°	77.5°	77.5°
Valve lift intake	10mm	10mm	10mm	10mm	10mm	10mm	12.8mm
Valve lift exhaust	10mm	10mm	10mm	10mm	10mm	10mm	10mm

ACKNOWLEDGEMENTS

THE AUTHOR

Grateful thanks are due to the following people for their help: Roger Bray, Jeff Moyes, Porsche Club GB, Fred Hampton, Mike Smith, Barry Curtis, Bob Garretson, George Shetliffe, Robert Coucher, Peter Stevens, Klaus Parr, Liz Harvey and Steve Kevlin.

THE EDITOR

For allowing their splendid 356s to be photographed for this book, sincere appreciation is due to the following: Porsche AG in Stuttgart (1950 Gmünd coupé and 1964 Carrera 2), Porsche Cars GB (1951 cabriolet and 1957 Speedster), AFN Porsche (1951 coupé, 1960 coupé and 1962 cabriolet), John Farrer (1954 coupé), John Paterack (1952 America Roadster), Paul and Janet Hough (1955 cabriolet), Colin Dexter (1955 coupé), Tim Dawson (1956 coupé), Steve Earl (1957 cabriolet), John Hearn (1958 coupé), Tom Freitag (1958 Convertible D), David Edelstein (1958 Roadster), Mike Smith (1959 Carrera GT), David Griffin (1964 coupé) and Bill Stephens (1964 cabriolet).

   Guidance in locating cars was provided by Fred Hampton, Jeff Moyes and Nate Cantwell. Rowan Isaac took the majority of the photographs, but the work of Dieter Rebmann, David Fetherston, Laurence Meredith, Dennis Adler and Fred Hampton is also featured.